"THE DEEP STATE
VERSUS
PRESIDENT TRUMP."

"An eye for an eye will only make the whole world blind."— Mahatma Gandhi

"Without assessing whether war does harm or good, we have found its cause in desire / craving / ambition which are the greatest causes of evil in individuals and states." — Plato's Republic, Book II

"Darkness cannot drive out darkness: only light can do that. Hate cannot drive out hate: only love can do that." — Martin Luther King

A skilful (commander) strikes a decisive blow, and stops. He does not dare (by continuing his operations) to assert and complete his mastery. He will strike the blow, but will be on his guard against being vain or boastful or arrogant in consequence of it. He strikes it as a matter of necessity; he strikes it, but not from a wish for mastery. — Lao Tzu

"You can bomb the world to pieces, you can't bomb it into peace"— Michael Franti

"When the power of love overcomes the love of power, the world will know peace."— Jimi Hendrix

"Imagine there's no countries
It isn't hard to do
Nothing to kill or die for
And no religion too
Imagine all the people
Living life in peace." — John Lennon

"The best fighter is never angry." — Lao Tzu

"Peace is always beautiful." — Walt Whitman

Wild Pelican Press LLC
Lady Lake, Florida

First Edition

3 2 1

to contact author by email:

BartAmericaFirst@gmail.com

I DEDICATE THIS BOOK TO

PRESIDENT DONALD TRUMP

AND TO US DEPLORABLES

WHO KNEW HE WOULD BE

AN EXCELLENT PRESIDENT.

MAY HE HAVE

EIGHT SUCCESSFUL YEARS AS POTUS.

CHAPTER ONE

WHY THE DEEP STATE IS ATTACKING
PRESIDENT DONALD TRUMP

On my way back to my home in Florida from Ireland, I had long layover in Heathrow. I hobbled over to a Costa where I got a delicious heated sandwich. Sitting down, I found myself at a table with a young American who told me he was with Army Intelligence. I asked a perfunctory question about whether he preferred the CIA or the FBI and he told me the FBI were very cooperative whereas the CIA was not. Our conversation rattled around looking for a theme for a couple of minutes and hit upon the crazy responses to President Trump's election.

SNOWFLAKES AND PHDs

He couldn't believe how crazily people were reacting to the president, and neither could I.   He told me about a fellow Intelligence Officer who was enrolled at a large private university and the president had sent each of the students an email.   It read: under the circumstances of this election, many of you are undoubtedly very upset. We offer counselling services for those who would like to sign up. We both laughed heartily. What a joke! The nation elects a new president and universities are offering counseling services?

I then told him I was a Ph.D. in philosophy and had written two books on Trump. I was one of the only two Ph.D.'s whom I knew in the entire country who supported Trump and voted for him. I'm a professor Emeritus with good credentials in my field. I'd already lost several "friends" because of my support for the President. I was not only amazed at how hateful a couple of professional friends had become, but I was amazed on how none of them saw through the propaganda barrage that Hilliar and Soros were putting out on the CNN (Clinton News Network). These were educated and established professors who were trained in philosophy to look beneath the appearances and discover reality. Instead, they were friggin' snowflakes, one of them even refusing to meet me because he said he "was a man of peace" and I had voted for Trump. What did he think President Trump was? The fact is, Candidate Trump was the candidate of Peace and Prosperity and Candidate Hilliar was the candidate of the warmonger neoconservatives. Had she won we would likely already be in a nuclear war with Russia, which is why many of us "deplorables" enthusiastically voted for Trump.

I asked him how his fellow Intelligence Officers in the Army were with Donald Trump being President. He looked puzzled and then laughed. "Oh," he said, "do you mean do they accept the Donald as their President?" Something like that, I said, and he laughed. "I can't believe all the crying snowflake women who marched with signs saying 'Trump is not my president.'" What country are they in? If they are in America and are Americans, sorry, their president is Donald Trump. More shared laughter.

We then began talking about the protestors who were getting paid $15/per hour to demonstrate against President Trump. I told him that those who were paying for these demonstrations ought to be jailed for sedition and treason. He agreed and then left for his gate.

WHY THE ESTABLISHMENT HATES PRESIDENT TRUMP

It is puzzling why the Establishment and Establishment politicians hate President Trump. The hate began when he was elected. He hadn't even done anything. One day into being President-elect Trump and the Establishment--- including Hilliar, Soros, Michael Moore and many so called "progressives" hated him.

I was very puzzled. I recalled when the second George Bush beat Al Gore. It was a contested election. The two teams were as diametrically opposed as Black and White. George Bush, the rich cocaine addict who had gone AWOL from the National Guard, had his drunken driving record suppressed, and was in the pocket of the Oil Industry. Al Gore, the standard bearer of environmental values, the Pied Piper warning us all about Global Warming, the deadly opponent of the Oil and Coal Industries. Eventually the Supreme Court stepped in and in an obscene decision gave the presidency to George Bush II. It was disgusting, a complete undermining of what democracy stood for. The recount was not finished in Florida but the Supremes came on stage and ended it.

But there were no "10000" women marches, there were no Michael Moore's promising a 100 days of rebellion against Bush II, there were no campaigns that pumped up the slogan "He's Not My President." If there ever were an election that demanded protest from the people, it was the illegitimate coronation of Bush II. The streets were silent. George Soros wasn't organizing "spontaneous" rallies in all the major cities. The transfer of power went smoothly. Bush II's inaugural wasn't memorable except for its lack of demonstrators and peacefulness. Why has Trump's been treated so differently?

This is an important question. It gets to the core of "what's going on." What's going on is that the Deep State, comprized of the neoconservatives and elements of the Intelligence agencies, are extremely threatened by President Trump. That still leaves unanswered the question "Why?"

He won the election, fair and square, and beat Hilliar at her own game. Why the hatred? Why the continuing demonstrations? Why the bleeping snowflakes and whining Ph.D.s?

One threat that a President Trump will embrace a peaceful approach to world politics. Except for defeating ISIS, Trump will withdraw military units from all over the world, close US military bases, and not play the "Global Cop" role played by Bill Clinton, George Bush, Barack Obama, and Secretary of State Hilliar. He is coming down the pike as a President of Peace and Prosperity. That always helps the little guy, who is the one put into a uniform and flown over to some Valley of Death like Afghanistan to return home under a flag or in a wheel chair. But it doesn't help the neocons who like to fight wars from behind their Washington DC desks or the military-industrial establishment which makes big money from war. The little guy, we average deplorables, did put Candidate Trump in office but it is the Deep State, compromising Obama and Hilliar and the CIA and the military-industrial complex and the neoconservatives who lose out in a peaceful world and so are attacking President Donald Trump.

Yet even this explanation, which seems to make good sense, doesn't answer the question "why Trump?" The reason is that Barack Obama came in as a peace candidate. He even had a Nobel Peace Prize under his arm when he entered the White House. Yet no one gave Obama a hard time or demonstrated in the streets or threatened to assassinate him. Why is the Deep State attacking President Trump when it didn't attack President Obama? What is the difference?

THE PUZZLE OF THE OBAMA ADMINISTRATION

The Obama administration was a puzzle. He came in as an anti-war candidate, pro "shovel-ready jobs" and promising to end the Bush tax cuts for the very wealthy. He broke each of those campaign promises. He was extremely pro-war: sent 50K American men and women into the Hell Hole of the Valley of Death called "Afghanistan." He obliterated Libya and oversaw the assassination of President Kaddafi. In a rather hypocritical moment during a panel discussion, he admitted he was wrong and that there were no "shovel-ready" jobs which was an obvious lie as the US infrastructure of highways and bridges was falling apart. He even extended the Bush tax cuts in a secret meeting with Republicans while Nancy Pelosi found out about it only later that evening at a White House reception. In short, he did a huge turnabout, betraying his campaign promises, acting to make the rich richer, and creating hundreds of thousands of war refugees across the Middle East. What happened to Obama? There are two theories.

The first is that he's a slick snake oil salesman, saying whatever is needed to get votes. Since I voted for him the first time around I did not want to believe that. He sounded so sincere and he'd written that great book, "The

Audacity of Hope," that both my wife and I were confident he was "for real." I had friends who disagreed. Obama's first cabinet picks were worrisome but I rationalized them by saying that he was picking people, like Hilliar, who could accomplish his programs: insiders who were "can do" people.

The second theory is that he was coerced into giving up his campaign promises and working for the neoconservatives, the Establishment, and the War Machine. The coercion idea is indeed plausible. The FBI undoubtedly knew that Obama was having affairs and was not the "solid family man" he pretended to be. He would eventually go so far out of his lane that he would have a love child with Beyoncé, though that occurred later. Furthermore, there's the old story we told each other in Ireland: after a new president took the oath of office, a special unique group of secret service affiliates took the president aside into a audio-visual bunker just under the steps where he took his oath of office. They proceeded to show him twelve minutes of video (with sound). In Obama's case, they first showed him naked and writhing with a beautiful black woman who was not Michelle. That took two minutes. The next eight minutes were scenes of the JFK assassination from different angles, showing the shooters on the Grassy Knoll and JFK's brains obviously being blown out with bullets coming from the front of his vehicle. The final two minutes included short videos of his children going to school in DC and photographs of horrible car accidents on the same streets. In short, for Obama to have kept his campaign promises would risk his reputation as a family man, his own life, and the lives of his children. He could hardly do otherwise than he did: overthrow his campaign promises for peace. He would become, as he did, an effective tool of the War Machine. `

Which theory is correct? For a time I favored the second theory, that he was coerced into violating his campaign promises. For one thing, he was so believable as the Candidate of Hope and Change. I only lately discovered there is a darker side to his character, one which fits with his having a love child outside of his marriage and, in general, being a man with no integrity but only ambition.

THE MILITARY INDUSTRIAL COMPLEX VETTED CANDIDATE OBAMA AND FOUND HIM PRO WAR

Being an investigative journalist is hard work and can even be dangerous. I cut my teeth on the profession with an established investigative journalist in Washington D.C., Ed Roeder. His name did create fear in the hearts of some supreme court nominees who didn't make it, thanks to Ed's digging through the history pile of old statements and speeches. We only did one piece together, but I was proud of it. I had the first byline, and I had done more work on it than Ed. It appeared in the Village Voice when the Voice was more prone to doing serious pieces.

Why I mention investigative journalism is because an investigative journalist solved the puzzle above: was Obama a slick snake oil salesman? Or was he coerced? It turns out I was wrong. Obama had taken all of us for a ride in the 2008 election.

Obama's pathetic attempts to explain his own inadequacies has often been underwhelming. Consider what William Blum points out: "On numerous occasions, in reply to a question about why his administration has not prosecuted the Bush-Cheney gang for mass murder, torture and other war crimes, former law professor Obama has stated: "I prefer to look forward rather than backwards." To make his point painfully clear, Blum continues: "Picture a defendant before a judge asking to be found innocent of any crime on such grounds "["Obama: Out of Many Sides of His Mouth," July 10, 2016: Independent Investigative Journalism Since 1995]. That Obama can be so banal does show he was a snake oil salesman. The investigative work of Nicolas J.S. Davies does. In the article "Vetting Warmonger Obama For Senate POTUS," published in Z Magazine on April 17, 2012, Davies writes:

> The U.S. system of legalized bribery ensures that candidates pass a rigorous program of ideological tests before they get anywhere near a seat in the U.S. Senate, let alone the White House. These tests take place in conversations over many years, as Lester Crown described to the Chicago Jewish News, and in endless hours of grueling calls and meetings to solicit bribes from wealthy Americans. The thoroughness and the personal nature of this process stands in stark contrast to the slick public relations campaign by which a candidate like Obama is eventually introduced to the American public.
>
> From his first interview with Lester Crown in Newton Minow's office in 1989 and throughout their 20-year relationship, Obama had to establish his credentials as a true believer in the ideology of American economic and military power. The backing of the Crown family then became an important and recognized signal to other military-industrial power brokers that Obama had passed scrutiny and could be relied on to serve their interests as president.

In short, Obama had passed the vetting process and was "one of the team" of warmongers. He then went forth, became president, and proceeded to promulgate war, death and destruction.

EXPLANATION OF WHY THE DEEP STATE IS ATTACKING PRESIDENT TRUMP AND DIDN'T ATTACK OBAMA

This explains why the Deep State did not attack Obama but is mercilessly attacking President Donald Trump and began as soon as he was elected. President Trump has not passed the "warmonger" test. He is a man who can carry out his promises, as he has been doing. When Obama said he was a president interested in creating peace in Afghanistan, the Deep State was comfortable knowing it was only campaign rhetoric. When Candidate Trump said he was in favor of peace with Russia, the Deep State didn't worry since it knew warmonger Hilliar was going to win the election. When she didn't, the Deep State faced its first American opponent since Abraham Lincoln. What to do with President Trump? The Deep State has not lost control of the foreign policy of the nation in any of our lifetimes. There are only two options: impeach him or assassinate him.

The Deep State includes National Security Agency, the CIA,, all the neocons, powerful politicians including John

McCain, who has been ruthlessly opposed to Trump and set himself up as the leader of the Republican Senators who oppose President Trump. These people are not playing around. They are and will do whatever they can to remove Donald Trump from the presidency.

THE LONG REACH OF THE DEEP STATE

They are also very influential. On this page, had I more four thousand dollars to spend for copyrights, I would have put images of the covers of The Economist, Time Magazine, and Bloomberg Businessweek. (To use the Business Week cover in your book will be $1,995. Let me know if you want it. [I thanked him and said I didn't.]) Now these are important and influential magazines that charge dear to put images of their covers in a book. The front covers as I write this are extremely disparaging of President Trump and his administration. The Economist has, all in red, an image of President Trump throwing a firebomb. Time magazine has a picture of Steve Bannon, Chief White House Strategist, with the "title" of "The Great Manipulator." Bloomberg Businessweek has a picture of President Donald Trump holding a signed executive order before the camera while sitting at the table where he had just signed it. You see the black folder, his signature, and then the words (in parenthesis): "Insert hastily drafted, legally dubious, economically destabilizing executive order here."

These are three top US magazines and each is influential. One is a widely read business magazine, one is the widely read Time magazine, and the third is the prestigious economic magazine, the Economist. This exhibits the reach of the Deep State and shows its hatred of President Donald Trump. The Deep State will do anything to discredit him. In our nation, which has just elected Candidate Donald Trump as its Supreme Commander-in-Chief, this is obscene.

The Deep State also has the puppet strings for actors and actresses and high-profile media people. Just this week (ending on 2/3/2017) Whoopi Goldberg equated President Donald Trump and his supporters to Islamic terrorists in the middle of her popular talk show. And in front of a massive television audience on January 21st, aging pop star Madonna called for people to "blow up" the White House and assassinate Trump. This is beyond strange and reveals the reach of the Deep State.

This propaganda manipulated by the Deep State is causing havoc for the secret service. Just this week the Secret Service is dealing with over 1200 Tweets calling for President Trump's assassination: the U.S. Secret Service field office in Louisville is still investigating the tweet sent by Heather Lowrey, according to special agent Richard Ferretti. It said, "If someone was cruel enough to assassinate MLK, maybe someone will be kind enough to assassinate Trump. #bekind #trump #lovetrumpshate," according to a screenshot provided to the Courier-Journal.

Lowrey could have violated United States Code Title 18, Section 871, "Threats Against President and Successors to the Presidency," which prohibits knowingly and willfully mailing or otherwise making "any threat to take the life of, to kidnap, or to inflict bodily harm upon the President of the United States." The charge, a Class E felony, is punishable by at least one year in prison and a maximum of five years.

 "Think twice before they [you] send it out," he said. "We are definitely monitoring social media."

Yet even US Senators are getting into the "screw over" Trump act. Recent news that John McCain and Lindsey Graham made a trip to Ukraine in early January 2017 was rather surprising. What is even more surprising is this commentary from Lindsey Graham and John McCain, made in the presence of Ukraine's President Poroshenko on the front lines of the Ukraine civil war, comments which seems to fly directly in the face of Donald Trump's approach to Russia:

Urging a restart of the stalled Ukrainian civil war, here's what Lindsey Graham had to say: "Your fight is our fight, 2017 will be the year of offense. All of us will go back to Washington and we will push the case against Russia. Enough of a Russian aggression. It is time for them to pay a heavier price.

"Our fight is not with the Russian people but with Putin. Our promise to you is to take your cause to Washington, inform the American people of your bravery and make the case against Putin to the world."

John McCain had this to say: "I believe you will win. I am convinced you will win and we will do everything we can to provide you with what you need to win. We have succeeded not because of equipment but because of your courage.

So I thank you and the world is watching and the world is watching because we cannot allow Vladimir Putin to succeed here because if he succeeds here, he will succeed in other countries."

Given that some theorize that actions taken by former Assistant Secretary of State for European and Eurasian Affairs at the U.S. Department of State, Victoria Nuland, may have engineered the regime change in Ukraine, the comments by both Graham and McCain seem particularly malevolent since they obviously are not making any kind of personal sacrifice in restarting this conflict.

What is even more interesting is a little-known federal law called the Logan Act, dating back to 1799, which reads as follows:

> "Any citizen of the United States, wherever he may be, who, without authority of the United States, directly or indirectly commences or carries on any correspondence or intercourse with any foreign government or any officer or agent thereof, with intent to influence the measures or conduct of any foreign government or of any officer or agent thereof, in relation to any disputes or controversies with the United States, or to defeat the measures of the United States, shall be fined under this title or imprisoned not more than three years, or both."

Perhaps it is time for President Trump to protect himself from these two renegade Senators and jail them for a couple of years. All Americans are equal under the law, right?

CHAPTER TWO

AN ALTERNATIVE VIEW OF THE ACADEMY AND TRUMP

This country may be torn and split by the election of President Donald Trump, but the professional community of philosophy Ph.D.s is united: Trump should not be POTUS. Our own association, the American Philosophical Association, issued a terse statement on the election:

The board of officers of the APA has voted unanimously to issue the following statement:

Leading up to the United States presidential election one month ago and in the weeks since, the nation has experienced increasingly divisive rhetoric and a rise in bias-based attacks on members of vulnerable groups. In light of this polarized post-election climate, the board of officers of the American Philosophical Association reaffirms the association's core values of inclusion and diversity, open and respectful dialogue, and academic freedom.

The board of officers further commits to continue working to ensure that all in the philosophical community and beyond have the opportunity to study, work, and engage in free inquiry across cultural, linguistic, and other social boundaries. Today, philosophy and other humanistic disciplines remain fundamental to our nation's most deeply held ideals of justice and freedom of expression, and as such, the work of philosophers and humanists is needed now more than ever.

"Building on the commitments expressed in the statement above and recognizing that spaces where many philosophers work—schools, colleges, and universities—have experienced reported examples of increased intolerance, upcoming APA meetings will include a number of sessions addressing issues of inclusion and diversity, open and respectful dialogue, and academic freedom.

"Links to a selection of these sessions, which have been organized by various groups including APA committees, program committees for their respective meetings, and affiliate groups, appear below. Full details of these sessions, plus information on many other sessions touching on topics relevant to the post-election context, are available in the meeting programs."

I want to emphasize a key sentence that impacts me and you in your non-philosophy academic profession: *In light of this polarized post-election climate, the board of officers of the American Philosophical Association reaffirms the association's core values of inclusion and diversity, open and respectful dialogue, and academic freedom.*

In my own PhD life during the election period, I have been ill-treated by professional colleagues: shunned, shamed, and not even brought into the conversation. That's why meeting another PhD on the trip from Orlando to Chicago was such a big deal. Can you imagine? One minute I think I'm the only Ph.D. in the country who voted for Trump (much less wrote two books on Trump). By the end of that flight I discover there are TWO OF US!!!!! Glory be!

On my little United napkin, I wrote the beginning of an outline of why professors were so messed up not to realize Trump would win and, worse, not to know by now that he will be the best president this country has had since George Washington, Thomas Jefferson, and Abraham Lincoln. (I omit FDR because FDR's presidency suffers from two very bad decisions on his part. First, he insisted on dividing Korea into North and South, setting the world (and America) up for the disastrous Korean War. Secondly, he didn't fight to keep his VP from his first three terms but allowed the Establishment chuck him [they didn't like his pacifism] for Harry Truman, the bigoted farm land who dropped two atomic bombs on Japan when he knew he was only doing it as a message to the Russians. I used to think well of Truman but now I am very sorry that Dewey didn't win.)

The outline from my napkin fleshed out with thoughts:

1) Professors make so much money they never have to worry about where their next meal will come from. Most of them get their checks automatically deposited into their bank accounts, so if they use <u>credit cards</u> they never have to touch dirty lucre. That's not the main reason they don't give to beggars, though it's enough to stop them. The main five reasons they don't give out money to the needy street people are: (a) they are way **too selfish**; (b) they think the needy are *play-acting* to get money for drink and dope and don't realize that they are trying to get enough money to buy food for their kids for another day prior to the receipt of food stamps; (c) they are **embarrassed** that people would actually beg from anyone; (d) they are **afraid of street people** and so don't even look at them when the street people say to the wealthy academics walking by, "God bless you" {they should say "God have mercy on your shriveled up prune of what was once a healthy soul, you selfish pile of walking poop"); (e) since they don't know any street people personally, in their rarefied world **street people are like cardboard cutouts** or a role someone takes on a stage set, like "the little Match Girl" who dies and no one cares except for her siblings, her friends, her family, her dog, and all the people to whom she brought joy when she was alive.

2) Professors talk to each other and to those above them (deans, provosts, presidents, Bill and Hilliar Clinton, Barack Obama and Michelle). In their "research," which is for them a form of extensive

footnotes and constitutes mental masturbation (this is a technical term used in the academy and so not politically incorrect), they write for only about a dozen of people who will be able to understand and appreciate their intellectual bullshit. If you look at my resume, most of my early papers were like that. Some were so technically obtuse I was stunned when someone wanted to publish them. The worst ones were

A) "The Defeat of Utilitarian Generalization," Ethics 93, October, 1982: 22-38.
B) "Assessing Acts of Pollution," Upstream/Downstream: Issues in Environmental Ethics, ed. Donald Scherer (Philadelphia: Temple University Press, 1990): 180-204.
C) "Mitigating Our Consumption of Our Living Standard," Philosophy and Its Public Role: Essays in Ethics, Politics, Society and Culture, edited by William Aiken and John Haldane (St. Andrews, UK: Imprint Academic, 2004), pp. 135-148.
D) "Thalberg's Perception, Emotion, and Action," Philosophical Investigations Vol. 4, No. 1, Winter, 1981: 49-52.
E) "Egonsson's Interests, Utilitarianism, and Moral Standing," Ethics, July, 1992.
F) "Vinit Haksar's Indivisible Selves and Moral Practice," The Philosophical Quarterly, April, 1993.
G) "Fu and Wawrytko's Buddhist Ethics and Modern Society," Ethics, April, 1994: 683.

H) Crocker and Linden, 'The Ethics of Consumption,'"
Environmental Ethics, Vol. 22, Fall 2000: 329-332.

The world and my *non-academic life* would have been a
sweeter place had none of those articles been written or
published---each was published on paper and wasted
diminishing resources. An environmental activist friend in
Northern California tried to read (B). It gave him a
headache and he felt he was reading a long article about the
inner workings of a watch---and it was just too much
information.

The worst of the lot were (A), (B) and (C). Each could only
be properly understood by very bright people educated in
those narrow areas. My reputation would never have been
what it is now, however, without (A), which is an argument
of finely tuned proportions, a sliver-splitting argument,
made up with numbers from scratch, which showed that the
most famous book on utilitarianism at the time, David
Lyons' **Forms and Limits of Utilitarianism**, was
essentially mistaken because I had shown, in that article,
that his main argument was fallacious. What irony! We
became the best of friends---he was impressed with my
intellect and yet easy-going working class background,
which he shared, and he became one of my very top

references---and I was impressed by his great intellect and his easy-going and humble manner. If David Lyons thought I was good, then that was the end of the issue. I was good. I knew he was not only an incredibly good philosopher but a very good human being. Like me, he came up from a working class background. Unlike me, he had been a professional plumber, a union man, very pro-labor, and even now, as a top ranking faculty member on Boston University's Law faculty, he fights for graduate teaching assistant unions and offers his services pro bona wherever they might be needed. How can you not like such a compassionate and humble human being of great intellect and platinum reputation?

Anyway, my wife Marion made me promise to stop pouring my energy into writing stuff that would be only read by a handful of people, including graduate students, who would read my stuff not out of love or interest but only to "keep up with the research." So I did. You would probably notice when that happened if you spent way too much time with my resume. I stopped giving technical talks, e.g., on utilitarianism; stopped publishing theoretical bullshit papers. I didn't realize it would happen, since I was being invited to conferences everywhere, but those invitations immediately dried up when I began writing and talking about things that any articulate high-school student could understand and even see how it was relevant to her life. I was no longer a rising star but now a sinking moon. I was writing and speaking for the deplorables, though Hilliar hadn't named us that as of yet.

3) Professors love control. I did too. We like well-behaved classes, no jerks disrupting our classes (and we have our own ways of destroying them), faculty meetings in which we are respected, praise from the wider academic community in our own institutions, and excellent course evaluations. We are in control. We think we're underpaid? We go to the Associate Dean and present our case and likely the math will fall out our way and we'll get an "equity" raise. We need to take off ten days to speak at conferences and be a visiting professor? We talk nicely to our chairman and the dean if necessary and arrange audio-visual events and exams while we are travelling. We don't want to teach in the summer? No problem. We do want to teach in the summer? No problem. We want to teach only our favorite courses? No problem. We don't want to teach ethical theory because we think it is bullshit although that's what we are known for in the profession? No problem. We like being in control and certainly I did.

That academic love of control came face-to-face on November 8th with the fact that "our" candidate, overweight Hilliar Clinton, didn't win and the horrible Donald Trump won the election. We are not used to not getting what we want and so we threw fits. Our students, noticing that our examples demonstrated that it was "okay" to throw fits, did so. We gave them weeks off to recover, cancelled exams, offered cry-in sessions, and made sure their safe-spaces were safe from the reality that Donald Trump was now the President-elect. Two of our number were out of step---an old fart 74 years old professor over the hill and a charming and beautiful young woman untenured professor. Each had broken ranks with us. For the old one, we stopped all communication immediately. For the younger one, she better pray that Trump turns out okay or she'll never get tenure. We don't screw around with turncoats.

4) Professors, finally, are hard-nosed and scientifically oriented if nothing else. We don't believe in angels, demons, spirits, ghosts, fairies, druids, or any other of that shit. Very recently we all agreed with Descartes that nonhuman animals not only don't have any intelligence, they don't have feelings and never suffer pain or pleasure. Some wise-assed graduate student, somewhere in the huge academic community stretching across the English-speaking world, had the audacity to point out that parent animals recognized their young and, when they left their dens or caves or nests, remembered how to get home. Hmmmm…. That graduate student was likely flunked out but others began asking similar questions. Don't elephants grieve? Aren't the great apes much like us? How can we expect to learn from a psychological experiment on mice if they don't have similar psychologies to us---and if they do, God forbid, how can we justify our cruel experiments on them that end with our cutting off their heads and examining their nerve tissue for changes? Finally Peter Singer, a respected mutual friend of mine, came along, wrote **Animal Liberation**, and the rest is, as they say, history. Animals counted.

That didn't make any space for angels, fairies, or ghosts, none of whom could be publically verified. It was public verification that turned philosophy from an interesting subject that poets and professors of all sorts could enjoy (look at the early pre-1930 issues of Journal of Philosophy) into a high-wired tight-rope game of complex analytic reasoning that almost no one found interesting. Didn't matter to us, we were the philosophy professors and we knew. WE KNEW. We didn't just guess or believe popular fairytales. We knew that angels, fairies, and such were popular fantasies held by the unwashed deplorables.

That's when "magical realism" began. Magical realism is a written, photographic, video or film account of great specific accuracy and then some magic enters: the fairy, the ghost, the Holy Ghost, a spirt, whatever. That's why it's called *magical* realism: it is utter realism with these unverifiable elements floating in and out creating the magic. Stories with angels or divine deities appearing are magical realism. That means that my wife's book, **Grief Alchemy: A story of Hospice** (check out the reviews and summary on Amazon), is very much in the category of Magical Realism. My book on Trump is not. My poems are and I'll put one here that was published in Ireland and is mentioned in my curriculum vitae. Here it is:

A River Ran Through It

We moved to Limerick, to Clancy's Strand,

Where the view of the Shannon is really quite grand.

So imagine our shock when we came to find out

That Dublin wants the Shannon, tough luck for the trout.

Tough too for the salmon, and I understand,

I've seen how this works, in a foreign land

I lived by the salmon, for a decade or so,
And there's lots about rivers I've come to know.
Dubliners could care less, as they covet our water,
That there'll be death to trout and a salmon slaughter.

These river thieves want us to put our worries aside,
Claiming that the fish already have long since died.
Codswallop! Atlantic salmon still spawn upstream
So stop pretending, don't salmon blaspheme!

The blasphemy's in the plan to pipe water east
While fish and eels and birds get fleeced.
Dubliners let toilets and taps drip away--
This ain't gonna stop 'til they're made to pay.

Dublin's water system leaks 50%
And frankly we've had it, we're fully hell-bent
On keeping this water flowing naturally south

Where it glides peacefully from the Shannon's mouth.

So Dublin: hands off our water, quit your selfish gripes,
Sort out your plumbing; fix your broken pipes.
I've been overseas where river water is taken
The river shrinks to mud, her spirit forsaken.

Those who plunder the water don't give it a thought
It's just water to them and they don't care a naught
About a river that dies or the fish who can't swim
Through sludge and debris, the ending's quite grim:

A death that salmon and swans and people must reap;
And for the river herself: a sacrilege deep.
The Shannon's more than her water and fish, she's a being alive,
Where beautify and history and energy thrive.

She's a being who has her own life force
Older than druids, and for many the source

Of joy and solace for an entire lifetime.

She's not just bits to buy or to steal--that's why I'm

Sayin' respect her, she's sacred, she has an ancient existence,

To take her water, her blood, would be a monstrous grievance.

Her water's not mine, not yours, it doesn't belong to some banker,

It belongs to herself, a "river" we call her.

She's from the heart of our island, flows from bog and woodland,

Bearing the life-force of springs, she's the Ganges of Ireland.

Don't dare try to drain her, don't take her for a whore,

Or Danu will punish you and your family forevermore.

by Bart Gruzalski

from <u>Anthology for a River</u>, ed. Teri Murray

If you look at my academic resume (called a "curriculum vitae"), my articles on the consciousness of nonhuman animals were magical realism at the time of their publication but are now only realism. Things change yet everything remains the same: mountains, rivers, nonhuman animals, fairies, angels, miracles. It's a wonderfully amazing and changing universe outside the Ivory Tower.

To wrap up (4): academics could not verify any reason or fact that would suggest Trump could possible win the presidency and so he didn't. But he did. That throws us back to (3), to tantrums, to using our excess wealth (1) to try to defeat Trump after he won and to write articles on how Trump won only because of the Russians (2). A sad business. Grief that needed to get out but professors could never admit that they were wrong, much less that they needed to grieve. A horribly contorted version of sick sick realistic professionalism.

There are other ways of saying some of the above and I don't have any trust that my list is complete. When there's craziness as deep as we are experiencing amongst the Ivory Tower leaders and shakers, there's probably much more at stake---maybe their mothers didn't breast feed them or stopped too soon. Maybe televisions babysat them while their academic parents were writing long footnotes. Who knows? There is deep in their consciousness a failed integrity and a scared little child who has never been out playing by herself in the woods. No wonder they all have security systems and tell their children to wash their hands if they've even touched grass.

At this point this chapter is exactly 3000 words and therefore the preferred length of papers presented at the American Philosophical Society meetings that occur on the East Coast, the Midwest, and the West Coast annually. It'd be a more interesting paper than any of those papers currently pending inclusion on an APA program and would undoubtedly stimulate a powerful and reflective discussion, but no group of academics would allow it to be on the program. Maybe I should try---call it something like "An Alternative View of Academics and Trump," spread it out over twelve pages double-spaced, and then enter it. It would be interesting to see (a) whether it was accepted and (b) where it appeared on the program. If it were accepted, it would likely appear as the first symposium---most people wouldn't even be at the meeting yet---or at the last late Saturday symposium---most people would already be leaving. It should be at 2PM in the middle of the meetings, but do you think philosophers would invite such self-criticism, self-sarcasm and humor into the middle meeting of a program? I may try it depending on the schedule for submissions. Oh, I will have to take away the self-deprecating reference to the well-known philosopher David Lyons but I think the rest could stand. A little "poop" and "bullshit" would liven up an APA meeting. After all, one of the widest read books in philosophy, the late Harry Frankfurt's book **On Bullshit**, is a stunning example of great analytic philosophy combined with a subtle Oxfordian humor. It was on the Times best seller list longer than any other book in philosophy, even those written by the likes of Martha Nussbaum, a great publicizer of serious philosophy, John Rawls, and Robert Nozack.

For the record: if I do submit this chapter, more or less as it is, I want to tell the team of judges for inclusion in an APA program that this **paper urges philosophers to apply, in their own political thinking, an awareness between appearances and reality; logic;** and **to beware aware of the power of cognitive dissonance**. That the profession has sunk so low in its assessment of President-elect Donald Trump is both an **embarrassment and a sign that something is amiss**. Either as professors we are not practicing what we preach, which I think is the problem, or as professors we just don't know what to preach. Either way, **professional philosophers need a reality jolt and need to embrace a bit more of magic realism and a lot** less of uppity hard-nosed verificationism. **Humility would be a big help** in this exercise.

Finally, I want to say to those of you assessing this chapter for inclusion in a philosophy program, that it will obviously generate **some grand discussion** and should probably be the only paper in a symposium session to have **three commentators**. I insist, as part of my submission, that **one of them be the other Ph.D. I met on the plane to Chicago if she is willing**. The second of which, if he is willing, be a professor well known to all of you, **Professor Henry West**. Finally, I recommend that the third professor commentating be drawn from the following short list: **Professor Samuel Gorovitz, Professor David Lyons, Professor Martha Nussbaum, and Professor Walter Sinnott-Armstrong**. Each of these professors has the skill to tear my presentation to bits while focusing on the whole point of the paper, the sad condition of philosophy professors during and after the November 8th, 2016 election of Donald Trump.

Thank you for your consideration. **IF you choose this as a symposium paper, it could be published ahead of time in the Division's Proceedings and then I could adlib the argument, touching on all the major points and reading only this entire paragraph in closing.**

Regardless, though, this is an important chapter in what I believe is a very important book. How can this chapter be important? The last chapter was deadly ion target: an explanation of why the Deep State wants Donald Trump impeached or dead. That's worth knowing about. Who cares that a bunch of snowflake Ph.D.s are anti-Trump? How can that be important?

That's a good question and here's the answer: those in the Deep State who are plotting to impeach or murder the President look to the academy for support. The neoconservative movement began with Professor Leo Strauss, an important University of Chicago philosopher who specialized in the study of ancient Western texts. A lot of neoconservative arguments for various techniques to manipulate public opinion rest on arguments the neoconservatives think originate with Plato. The neoconservatives are, in fact, terrible academics but that's not the point. The point is that the neoconservatives and the entire Deep State look to the academy for legitimacy. And the academy is not letting them down. The active complicity of the academy and its Ph.D.s is deeply relevant to the major theme of this book.

CHAPTER THREE

THE "COLOR REVOLUTION" UNDER WAY IN THE USA

A Russian joke goes like this: "*Question: why can there be no color revolution in the United States? Answer: because there are no US Embassies in the United States.*"

Funny, maybe, but factually wrong: I believe that a color revolution *is* being attempted in the USA right now.

Politico magazine seems to feel the same way (see their recent cover).

While I did predict that "The USA are about to face the worst crisis of their history" as far back as October of last year, a month before the elections, I have to admit that I am surprised and amazed at the magnitude of struggle which we see taking place before our eyes. It is now clear that the Neocons did declare war on Trump and some, like Paul Craig Roberts, believe that Trump has now returned them the favor. I sure hope that he is right.

Let's look at one telling example:

US intelligence agencies are now investigating their own boss! Yes, according to recent reports, the FBI, CIA, National Security Agency and

Treasury Department are now investigating the telephone conversations between General Flynn and the Russian ambassador Sergey Kislyk. According to Wikipedia, General Flynn is the former

- Director of the Defense Intelligence Agency
- Joint Functional Component Command for Intelligence, Surveillance and Reconnaissance
- Chair of the Military Intelligence Board
- Assistant Director of National Intelligence
- Senior intelligence officer for the Joint Special Operations Command.

He is also Trump's National Security Advisor. In other words, his security clearance is stratospherically high and he will soon become the boss of all the US intelligence services. And yet, these very same intelligence services are investigating him for his contacts with the Russian Ambassador. *That is absolutely amazing.* Even in the bad old Soviet Union, the putatively almighty KGB did not have the right to investigate a member of the Communist Party Central Committee without a special authorization of the Politburo (a big mistake, in my opinion, but never mind that). That roughly means that the top 500 members of the Soviet state could not be investigated by the KGB at all. Furthermore, such was the subordination of the KGB to the Party that for common criminal matters the KGB was barred from investigating any member of the entire Soviet Nomenklatura, roughly 3 million people (and even bigger mistake!).

But in the case of Flynn, several US security agencies can decide to investigate a man who by all standards ought to be considered at least in the top 5 US officials and who clearly has the trust of the new President. And that does not elicit any outrage, apparently.

By the same logic, the three letter agencies might as well investigate Trump for his telephone conversations with Vladimir Putin. Which, come to think of it, they might well do it soon…

This is all absolutely crazy because this is evidence that the US intelligence community as gone rogue and is now taking its orders from the Neocons and their deep state and not from the President and that these agencies are now acting against the interests of the new President.

In the meantime, the Soros crowd has already chosen a color: pink. We now are witnessing the "*pussyhat revolution.*" And if you think that this is just a small fringe of lunatic feminists, you would be quite wrong. For the truly lunatic feminists the "subtle" hint about their "*pussyhat revolution*" is too subtle, so they prefer making their statement less ambiguous as the image showing a woman dressed as a bright pink Vulva shows (investigate online).

This would all be rather funny, in a nauseating way I suppose, if it wasn't for the fact that the media, Congress and Hollywood are fully behind this "100 days of Resistance to Trump" which began by a, quote, "queer dance party" at Mike Pence's house.

This would be rather hilarious, if it was not for all gravitas with which the corporate media is treating these otherwise rather pathetic "protests".

Watch how MCNBS's talking head blissfully reporting this event:

Listen carefully to what Moore says at 2:00. He says that they will "celebrate the fact that Obama is still the President of the United States" and the presstitute replies to him, "yes he is" not once, but twice. What are they talking about?! The *fact* that Obama is still the President?!

How is it that Homeland Security and the FBI are not investigating MCNBC and Moore for rebellion and sedition?

So far, the protests have not been too large, but they did occur in various US cities and they were well covered by the media:

Make no mistake, such protest are no more spontaneous than the ones in the Ukraine.

Somebody is paying for all this, somebody is organizing it all. And they are using their full bag of tricks. One more example:

Remember the pretty face of Nayirah, the Kuwaiti nurse who told Congress that she had witnessed Iraqi soldiers tossing our babies from Kuwaiti incubators (and who later turned out to be the daughter of Saud Al-Sabah, the Kuwaiti ambassador to the United States)? Do you remember the pretty face of Neda, who "died on TV" in Iran? Well, let me introduce you to Bana Alabe, who wrote a letter to President Trump and, of course, the media got hold of the latter and now she is the "face of the Syrian children".

Want even more proof?
Okay, take a look at a sampling of anti-Trump caricatures and cartoons complied by the excellent

Colonel Cassad. Some of them are quite remarkable. From this nauseating collection, I will discuss just two:

The first one shows a Trump hand puppet in Putin's hand saying that he is not influenced by anyone. This cartoon clearly accuses Trump of being in the hands of Putin. The second one makes Trump the heir to Adolf Hitler and strongly suggests that Trump might want to restart Auschwitz. Translated into plain English this sends a double message: Trump is not the legitimate President of the USA and Trump is the ultimate Evil.

**This goes far beyond the kind of satire previous Presidents have ever been subjected to.**
My purpose in listing all the examples above is to suggest the following: _**far from having accepted defeat, the Neocons and the US deep state have decided, as they always do, to double-down and they are now embarking on a full-scale "color revolution" which will only end**_

with the impeachment, overthrowal or death of Donald Trump.

One of the most amazing features of this color revolution against Trump is the fact that those behind it *don't give a damn about the damage that their war against Trump does to the institution of the President of the United States and, really, to the United States as a whole.* That damage is, indeed, immense and the bottom line is this: **President Trump is in <u>immense</u> danger of being overthrown and his <u>only</u> hope for survival is to strike back hard and fast.**

The other amazing thing is the ugly role Britain plays in this process: all the worst filth against Trump is always eventually traced back right to the UK. How come? Simple. Do you recall how, formally at least, the CIA and NSA did not have the right to spy on US nationals and the British MI6 and GCHQ had no right to spy on British nationals. Both sides found an easy way out: they simply traded services: the CIA and

NSA spied on Brits, the MI6 and GCHQ spied on Americans, and then they simply traded the data between "partners" (it appears that since Obama came to power all these measures have now become outdated and everybody is free to spy on whomever the hell they want, including their own nationals). The US Neocons and the US deep state are now using the British special services to produce a stream of filth against Trump which they then report as "intelligence" and which then can be used by Congress as a basis for an investigation. Nice, simple and effective.

The bottom line is this: President Trump is in <u>immense</u> danger of being overthrown and his <u>only</u> hope for survival is to strike back hard and fast.

<u>Can he do that?</u>
Until now I have suggested several times that Trump deal with the US Neocons the way Putin dealt with the oligarchs in Russia: get them on

charges of tax evasion, corruption, conspiracy, obstruction of justice, etc. All that good stuff which the US deep state has been doing for years. The Pentagon and the Three Letter Agencies are probably the most corrupt entities on the planet and since they have never been challenged, never mind punished, for their corruption they must have become fantastically complacent about how they were doing things, essentially counting on the White House to bail them out in case of problems. The main weapon used by these circles are the numerous secrecy laws which protect them from public and Congressional scrutiny. But here Trump can use his most powerful card: General Flynn who, as former director of the DIA and current National Security Advisor to the President will have total access. And if he doesn't – he can create it, if needed by sending special forces to ensure "collaboration".

However, I am now beginning to think that this might not be enough. Trump has a

much more powerful weapon he can unleash against the Neocon: 9/11.

Whether Trump knew about it before or not, he is now advised by people like Flynn who must have known for years that 9/11 was in inside job. And if the actual number of people directly implicated in the 9/11 operation itself was relatively small, the number of people which put their full moral and political credibility behind the 9/11 official narrative is immense. **Let me put it this way: while 9/11 was a US "deep state" operation (probably subcontracted for execution to the Israelis), <u>the entire Washington "swamp" has been since "9/11 accomplice after the fact" by helping to maintain the cover-up</u>. If this is brought into light, then <u>thousands</u> of political careers are going to crash and burn into the scandal.**

9/11 was a collective crime *par excellence*. A few men actually executed it, but then thousands, possibly tens of thousands, have used their position to execute the cover-up and to prevent any real investigation. They are ALL guilty of obstruction of justice. By opening a new investigation into 911, but one run by the Justice Department and NOT by Congress, Trump could literally place a "political handgun" next to the head of each politician and threaten to pull the trigger if he does not immediately give up on trying to overthrow Trump.

What Trump needs for that is a 100% trusted and 100% faithful men as the director of the FBI, a man with *"clean hands, a cool head and a burning heart"* (to use the expression of the founder of the Soviet Secret Police, Felix Dzerzhinsky). This man will immediately find himself in physical danger so he will have to be a man of great personal courage and determination. And, of course, this "man" could be a woman (a US equivalent of the Russian prosecutor, Natalia Poklonskaia).

I fully understand that danger of what I am suggesting as any use of the "9/11 weapon" will, of course, result in an immense counter-attack by the Neocons and the deep state. But here is the deal: the latter are already dead set in impeaching, overthrowing or murdering Donald Trump. And, as Putin once said in an interview, "if you know that a fight is inevitable, then strike first!".

You think that all is this over the top? Consider what is at stake.

First, at the very least, the Trump Presidency itself: the Neocons and the US deep state will not let Trump implement his campaign promises and program. Instead they will sabotage, ridicule and misrepresent everything he does, even if this is a big success.

Second, it appears that Congress now has the pretext to open several different congressional investigations into Donald Trump. If that is the case, it will be easy for Congress to blackmail Trump and constantly threaten him with political retaliation if he does not "get with the program".

Third, the rabid persecution of Trump by the Neocons and the deep state is weakening the institution of the Presidency. For example, the latest crazy notion floated by some politicians is to *"prohibit the President of the United States from using nuclear weapons without congressional authorization except when the United States is under nuclear attack."* From a technical point of view, this is nonsense, but what it does is send the following signal to the rest of the planet: ***"we, in Congress, believe that our Commander in Chief cannot be trusted with nuclear weapons."*** Never mind that they would trust Hillary with the same nukes and never mind that Trump could use only conventional weapons to trigger a global nuclear war anyway (by, for example, a conventional attack on the Kremlin), what they are saying is that the US President is a lunatic that cannot be trusted. How can they then expect him to be taken seriously on <u>any</u> topic?

Fourth, can you just imagine what will happen if the anti-Trump forces are successful?! Not only will democracy be totally and terminally crushed inside the USA, but the risks of war, including nuclear, will simply go through the roof.

**There is much more at stake here than just petty US politics.**
Every time I think of Trump and every time I look at the news I always come back to the same anguished thought: _**will Trump have the intelligence to realize the fact that he is under attack and will he have the courage to strike back hard enough?**_

I don't know.

I have a great deal of hopes for General Flynn. I am confident that he understands the picture perfectly and knows exactly what is going on. But I am not sure that he has enough pull with the rest of the armed forces to keep them on the right side should a crisis happen. Generally, "regular" military types don't like intelligence people. My hope is that Flynn has loyal allies at

SOCOM and JSOC as, at the end of the day, they will have the last say as to who occupies the White House. The good news here is that unlike regular military types, special forces and intelligence people are usually very close and used to work together (regular military types also dislike special forces). SOCOM and JSOC will also know how to make sure that the CIA doesn't go rogue.

**Last but not least, my biggest hope is that Trump will use the same weapon Putin used against the Russian elites: the support of the people.** But for that task, Twitter is simply not good enough. Trump needs to go the "RT route" and open his own TV channel. Of course, this will be very hard and time consuming, and he might have to begin with an Internet-based only channel, but as long as there is enough money there, he can make it happen. And, just like RT, it needs to be multi-national, politically diverse (including anti-Empire figures who do not support Trump) and include celebrities.

One of the many mistakes made by Yanukovich in the Ukraine was that he did not dare to use the legal instruments of power to stop the neo-Nazis. And to the degree that he used them, it was a disaster (like when the riot cops beat up student demonstrators). After listening to a few interviews of Yanukovich and of people near him during those crucial hours, it appears that Yanukovich simply did not feel that he had a moral right to use violence to suppress the street. We will never know if what truly held him back are moral principles or basic cowardice, but what is certain is that he betrayed his people and his country when he refused to defend <u>real</u> democracy and let the "street" take over replacing democracy with *ochlocracy* (mob rule). Of course, real ochlocracy does not exist, all mobs are always controlled by behind-the-scenes forces who unleash them just long enough to achieve their goals.

<u>The forces which are currently trying to impeach, overthrow or murder President Trump are a clear and present danger to the</u>

<u>*United States as a country and to the US*</u> <u>*Federal Republic.*</u> They are, to use a Russian word, a type of "non-system" opposition which does not want to accept the outcome of the elections and which by rejecting this outcome essentially oppose the entire political system.

I am not a US citizen (I could, but I refuse that citizenship on principle because I refuse to take the required oath of allegiance) and the only loyalty I owe the USA is the one of a guest: never to deliberately harm it in any way and to obey its laws. And yet it turns my stomach to see how easy it has been to turn millions of Americans against their own country.

I write a lot about russophobia on my blog, but I also *see a deep-seated "Americanophobia" or "USophobia" in the words and actions of those who today say that Trump is not their President. To them, their micro-identity as a "liberal" or as a "gay" or as "African-American" means more than the very basic fundamental principles upon which this country has been built.* When I see these crowds of Trump-bashers I see pure, seething hatred not of the AngloZionist Empire, or of a plutocracy masquerading as a democracy, but a hatred of what I would call the "simple America" or the "daily America" – the simple people amongst whom I have now lived for many years and learned to respect and appreciate and whom the Clinton-bots only think of as "deplorables".

It amazes me to see that the US pseudo-elites have as much hatred, contempt and fear of the American masses as the Russian pseudo-elites have hatred, contempt and fear of the Russian masses (the Russian equivalent or Hillary's "deplorables" would be a hard to pronounce for English speakers word "?????", roughly "cattle", "lumpen" or "rabble"). It amazes me to see that the very same people which have demonized Putin for years are now demonizing Trump using exactly the same methods. And if their own country has to go down in their struggle against the common people – so be it! These self-declared elites will have no compunction whatsoever to destroy the nation they have been parasitizing and exploiting for their own class interest. **They did just that to Russia exactly 100 years ago, in 1917. I sure hope that they will not get away with that again in 2017.**

CHAPTER FOUR

WHAT WE AS DEPLORABLES CAN DO TO DEFEND TRUMP AGAINST THIS ATTACK BY THE DEEP STATE

Our President and our democracy is under attack by a host of elites and easily manipulated snowflakes. There are three actions we can take that will help defend President Trump from this treasonous attack.

FIRST, sign petitions, write to the local newspaper, call in to the local radio station, call your Congressperson making it clear that we want a thorough investigation of 9/11.

SECOND, take the same actions but in order to motivate Homeland Security to put people like Michael Moore in jail for treason and sedition.

THIRD, we must make fun of the snowflake practices in the universities---"safe spaces" so people don't have to hear anything that upsets them; cancelled examinations because students are upset that Donald Trump is President; offers of counseling for those upset by the election. We should do this in letters to the editors and on call-in shows. The aim is to undermine the legitimacy of the university as a bulwark to support the Deep State in its plot to impeach or kill our President.

Transition

What you have just read is the point of my writing this book. I wanted to explain why the Deep State is attacking President Donald Trump and working for his impeachment or murder, it does not care which. I also wanted to explain the steps that the Trump administration can take to foil this attack and, finally, the steps that you, the reader, need to take to support President Donald Trump and to help insure that government of the people, by the people, and for the people shall not continue to flourish here in the United States.

The next chapters are background material you might not be aware of, and historical connections between the Trump administration and the presidency of George Washington. I begin with an annotated version of Candidate Trump's foreign policy address of April, 2016.

The material after that---about George Washington and President Trump's own plan for protecting the USA without violence---has been published in my book **The Moral Imperative of "America First!": Join November's Nonviolent Christian Revolt against America's Royalty.** It is deeply relevant in my first book on President Trump since the historically important election.

CHAPTER FIVE

DONALD J. TRUMP'S FOREIGN POLICY SPEECH

APRIL 27, 2016

In the following pages you will find Donald Trump's very important publicly available speech on foreign policy.   I have annotated the speech.

That means below Donald Trump's words I have comments that I hope will be of help to some readers for putting the speech in a larger context or elucidating something that might not be perfectly clear or providing an example of what is talked about in the text. ***My annotated comments will be italicized in bold like this sentence.*** There will be a line separating Trump's speech from my commentary. It has been my privilege to annotate the speech and I hope that you find the commentary helpful.

Thank you for the opportunity to speak to you, and thank you to the Center for the National Interest for honoring me with this invitation.

I would like to talk today about how to develop a new foreign policy direction for our country – one that replaces randomness with purpose, ideology with strategy, and chaos with peace.

It is time to shake the rust off of America's foreign policy. It's time to invite new voices and new visions into the fold.

The direction I will outline today will also return us to a timeless principle. My foreign policy will always put the interests of the American people, and American security, above all else. That will be the foundation of every decision that I will make.

America First will be the major and overriding theme of my administration.

The current foreign policy of the United States does appear random in its shifting focus from one country or hot spot to another, seems at best to reflect the ideology of the neoconservative movement which is closely tied with Israel and the AIPAC, and clearly is not doing anything to promote peace but has left chaos and suffering in Afghanistan, Iraq, Libya, and everywhere our president has approved military intervention. The visions that guide our current policy are dark. At best we are trying to satisfy Israel's desire to be the only power standing in the Middle East. None of our interventions in the Middle East have done anything but undermine American security. Our kneejerk support of Israel, though sending her arms, giving her $3Billion of our tax dollars every January, and covering her misdeeds with Vetoes in the Security Council of the United Nations, motivated bin Laden to attack us. To begin to develop a foreign policy that would focus on America first and the security of Americans would be novel. This is what Donald Trump will talk about in his speech.

But to chart our path forward, we must first briefly look back.

We have a lot to be proud of. In the 1940s we saved the world. The Greatest Generation beat back the Nazis and the Japanese Imperialists. Then we saved the world again, this time from totalitarian Communism. The Cold War lasted for decades, but we won.

Democrats and Republicans working together got Mr. Gorbachev to heed the words of President Reagan when he said: "tear down this wall."

History will not forget what we did.

Unfortunately, after the Cold War, our foreign policy veered badly off course. We failed to develop a new vision for a new time. In fact, as time went on, our foreign policy began to make less and less sense.

Logic was replaced with foolishness and arrogance, and this led to one foreign policy disaster after another.

The Korean War was the first war after WWII. It began because the North Koreans invaded South Korea and the UN called upon nations of the world to counter. The U.S. supplied 88% of the UN troops defending South Korea. It was a terribly bloody war of attrition that began on June 27, 1950. The fighting ended on July 27, 1953, when an <u>armistice</u> was signed. North Korea and South Korea are still technically at war since no peace treaty was ever signed.

The Korean tragedy was followed by the absolute folly of the Vietnam War. The American people rose up in protest of that immoral and unjustifiable war. After over 50,000 US troops were killed, the war ended in an ignominious defeat for the United States. The photographs of the last helicopter escaping from the American embassy shows people hanging on and then falling to their deaths. It was a photograph that burrowed itself into the American psyche.

We went from mistakes in Iraq to Egypt to Libya, to President Obama's line in the sand in Syria. Each of these actions have helped to throw the region into chaos, and gave ISIS the space it needs to grow and prosper.

It all began with the dangerous idea that we could make Western democracies out of countries that had no experience or interest in becoming a Western Democracy.

We tore up what institutions they had and then were surprised at what we unleashed. Civil war, religious fanaticism; thousands of American lives, and many trillions of dollars, were lost as a result. The vacuum was created that ISIS would fill. Iran, too, would rush in and fill the void, much to their unjust enrichment.   Our foreign policy is a complete and total disaster.

No vision, no purpose, no direction, no strategy.

We invaded Afghanistan to fight the Taliban in Afghanistan, yet the Taliban had not attacked

73

us on 9/11. Bin Laden was allegedly the brains behind that attack and was allegedly in territory controlled by the Taliban. The Taliban offered to turn bin Laden over to a third country if the US would offer evidence that he was responsible for 9/11. President Bush II refused and announced weeks in advance when we would begin the war, thus giving those who wanted to escape plenty of warning. We invaded a country that had defeated the Russians and likely contributed to the death of Alexander the Great. The type of guerilla-style fighting that Alexander faced during his Afghan campaign was described centuries later by the chronicler Plutarch, who compared Afghan tribesmen to a hydra-headed monster. as soon as Alexander cut off one head, three more would grow back in its place. As of October 7, the Afghan War has been going on for 15 years. More than 2,300 US troops have died there. The conflict has cost US taxpayers an estimated $686bn. Obama sent an additional 51, 000 military into this Valley of Death in 2009.

Today, I want to identify five main weaknesses in our foreign policy.

First, Our Resources Are Overextended
President Obama has weakened our military by weakening our economy. He's crippled us with wasteful spending, massive debt, low growth, a huge trade deficit and open borders.

Our manufacturing trade deficit with the world is now approaching $1 trillion a year. We're rebuilding other countries while weakening our own.

Ending the theft of American jobs will give us the resources we need to rebuild our military and regain our financial independence and strength.

I am the only person running for the Presidency who understands this problem and knows how to fix it.

Trump is a businessman and he understands how Obama has weakened our economy until it has reached a dire state. As Trump points out, our manufacturing trade deficit is

approaching $1trillion per year. Those
countries with which we have a trade deficit
are able to put more resources into their
economy and their infrastructures. We pay for
that with our trade deficit.

In addition to ending the theft of American
jobs though Bill Clinton's NAFTA which is the
worst trade agreement in history, Trump will
also add jobs to the economy that make 90,000
a year. These jobs are the "shovel ready" jobs
that Obama promised and then failed to
deliver. These jobs involve fixing our nation's
highways and bridges. As road builders and
bridge builders bring home their pay, the
butcher and baker and candle-stick maker will
also begin making decent wages again. As
money spreads though our communities, not
only will people feel better about themselves as
they ply their professions, but taxes will be
paid to local, state, and federal governments.

Secondly, our allies are not paying their fair share.

Our allies must contribute toward the financial, political and human costs of our tremendous security burden. But many of them are simply not doing so. They look at the United States as weak and forgiving and feel no obligation to honor their agreements with us.

In NATO, for instance, only 4 of 28 other member countries, besides America, are spending the minimum required 2% of GDP on defense.

We have spent trillions of dollars over time – on planes, missiles, ships, equipment – building up our military to provide a strong defense for Europe and Asia. The countries we are defending must pay for the cost of this defense – and, if not, the U.S. must be prepared to let these countries defend themselves.

The whole world will be safer if our allies do their part to support our common defense and security.

A Trump Administration will lead a free world that is properly armed and funded.

Donald Trump the businessman is acutely aware of when business cooperatives are financially successful or not. We are almost single-handedly supporting NATO and the defense of Europe. NATO is a cooperative with one primary funder: the USA.

And then there's the folly of giving a huge amount of money to Israel every January, as if Israel is a poor nation desperately in need of our aid. The Palestinians are desperately in need of our aid but get only a pittance when compared with what we give Israel: over $3 billion dollars every January.

If Hillary Clinton were elected president, that amount might well rise, since she has campaigned on the promise that she will nurture much stronger and closer ties to Israel.

Thirdly, our friends are beginning to think they can't depend on us.

We've had a president who dislikes our friends and bows to our enemies.

He negotiated a disastrous deal with Iran, and then we watched them ignore its terms, even before the ink was dry.

Iran cannot be allowed to have a nuclear weapon and, under a Trump Administration, will never be allowed to have a nuclear weapon.

All of this without even mentioning the humiliation of the United States with Iran's treatment of our ten captured sailors.

In negotiation, you must be willing to walk. The Iran deal, like so many of our worst agreements, is the result of not being willing to leave the table. When the other side knows you're not going to walk, it becomes absolutely impossible to win.

While I am among those who celebrate that we have a deal with Iran, Obama's deal was not well negotiated. Donald Trump, who knows how to negotiate, would have gotten us far better terms.

A Trump administration will be committed to insuring that Iran never gets a nuclear weapon.

Iran did make sure they got their propaganda from having captured ten US sailors with arms and ammunition. Five were on a boat that broke down and drifted into Iranian territorial waters. Their "capture" and the publicity surrounding it were more than was necessary, although I think the humiliation was the fact of the ten US service men being captured, not in anything that the Iranians did to them or to publicize their capture.

At the same time, your friends need to know that you will stick by the agreements that you have with them.

President Obama gutted our missile defense program, then abandoned our missile defense plans with Poland and the Czech Republic. He supported the ouster of a friendly regime in Egypt that had a longstanding peace treaty with Israel – and then helped bring the Muslim Brotherhood to power in its place.

Israel, our great friend and the one true Democracy in the Middle East, has been snubbed and criticized by an Administration that lacks moral clarity. Just a few days ago, Vice President Biden again criticized Israel – a force for justice and peace – for acting as an impediment to peace in the region.

President Obama has not been a friend to Israel. He has treated Iran with tender love and care and made it a great power in the Middle East – all at the expense of Israel, our other allies in the region and, critically, the United States.

We've picked fights with our oldest friends, and now they're starting to look elsewhere for help.

Fourth, our rivals no longer respect us.
In fact, they are just as confused as our allies, but an even bigger problem is that they don't take us seriously any more.

When President Obama landed in Cuba on Air Force One, no leader was there to meet or greet him – perhaps an incident without precedent in the long and prestigious history of the United States.

Then, amazingly, the same thing happened in Saudi Arabia -- it's called no respect.

These disrespectful welcomes of the President show that our status in the world is sinking fast. The most recent examples, China and most recently the Philippines.

Do you remember when the President made a long and expensive trip to Copenhagen, Denmark to get the Olympics for our country, and, after this unprecedented effort, it was announced that the United States came in fourth place? He should have known the result before making such an embarrassing commitment.

The list of humiliations goes on and on.

President Obama watches helplessly as North Korea increases its aggression and expands even further with its nuclear reach.

Our president has allowed China to continue its economic assault on American jobs and wealth, refusing to enforce trade rules – or apply the leverage on China necessary to rein in North Korea. He has even allowed China to steal government secrets with cyber attacks and engage in industrial espionage against the United States and its companies.

We've let our rivals and challengers think they can get away with anything.

If President Obama's goal had been to weaken America, he could not have done a better job.

The Philippines example is the most recent and the most outrageous. **Philippine President Rodrigo Duterte's vitriol against the United States took a negative turn in September when he called Barack Obama a "son of a whore." Almost a month later, he said President Barack Obama can "go to hell" and served notice to the US that the joint naval maneuvers "will be the last joint military exercise with US."**

Subsequently the Philippine President *went to China where he announced a complete break with the economic and military relationship with the US. He turned to China and to Russia to join together against the rest of the world. This was disrespect and significantly more, the destruction of a 70 year relationship between the US and the Philippines.*

Finally, America no longer has a clear understanding of our foreign policy goals.

Since the end of the Cold War and the break-up of the Soviet Union, we've lacked a coherent foreign policy. One day we're bombing Libya and getting rid of a dictator to foster democracy for civilians, the next day we are watching the same civilians suffer while that country falls apart.

We're a humanitarian nation. But the legacy of the Obama-Clinton interventions will be weakness, confusion, and disarray. We have made the Middle East more unstable and chaotic than ever before. We left Christians subject to intense persecution and even genocide. Our actions in Iraq, Libya and Syria have helped unleash ISIS.

And we're in a war against radical Islam, but President Obama won't even name the enemy! Hillary Clinton also refuses to say the words "radical Islam," even as she pushes for a massive increase in refugees.

After Secretary Clinton's failed intervention in Libya, Islamic terrorists in Benghazi took down our consulate and killed our ambassador and three brave Americans. Then, instead of taking charge that night, Hillary Clinton decided to go home and sleep! Incredible. Clinton blames it all on a video, an excuse that was a total lie. Our Ambassador was murdered and our Secretary of State misled the nation – and by the way, she was not awake to take that call at 3 o'clock in the morning.

And now ISIS is making millions of dollars a week selling Libyan oil.

Clinton's mismanagement of Benghazi is enough to indict her for allowing an ambassador to be killed. Her lie about the attack being caused by a video is sinful. There is nothing here but incompetence and cover-up, both grotesque. And then, in anger, Hillary had the nerve to beat on a table at the Benghazi hearing and shout, "What difference does it make?" meaning: the ambassador and three Americans are dead, they won't arise from the dead whatever we say here so what difference does it make? There's no point in discussing it any more, is there?

There is a point to one further discussion, one in front of a court at a trial for a Secretary of State who failed to protect American lives which was her first duty to the ambassador.

This will change when I am president.
To all our friends and allies, I say America is going to be strong again. America is going to be a reliable friend and ally again.

We're going to finally have a coherent foreign policy based upon American interests, and the shared interests of our allies.

We are getting out of the nation-building business, and instead focusing on creating stability in the world.

Our moments of greatest strength came when politics ended at the water's edge.

We need a new, rational American foreign policy, informed by the best minds and supported by both parties, as well as by our close allies.

This is how we won the Cold War, and it's how we will win our new and future struggles.

*Donald Trump's foreign policy speech
changes at this point. He begins focusing on
how he will create foreign policy.*

*No more nation-building, that ridiculous but
brutally destructive approach to the way we
tried to manage Iraq after laying waste to the
major cities outside of Baghdad. No more
flexing our "military muscle" and attacking
nations like Libya, which was Hilliar's attempt
to look more "presidential."*

*We need a foreign policy that represents all of
those in the Senate and House of
Representatives, one that is supported by all
the People. That is how we won the cold war,
as Trump says, and it is a winning strategy to
carry us into the future.*

First, we need a long-term plan to halt the spread and reach of radical Islam.
Containing the spread of radical Islam must be a major foreign policy goal of the United States. Events may require the use of military force. But it's also a philosophical struggle, like our long struggle in the Cold War.

In this we're going to be working very closely with our allies in the Muslim world, all of which are at risk from radical Islamic violence.

We should work together with any nation in the region that is threatened by the rise of radical Islam. But this has to be a two-way street – they must also be good to us and remember us and all we are doing for them.

The struggle against radical Islam also takes place in our homeland. There are scores of recent migrants inside our borders charged with terrorism. For every case known to the public, there are dozens more. We must stop importing extremism through senseless immigration policies.

A pause for reassessment will help us to prevent the next San Bernardino or worse -- all you have to do is look at the World Trade Center and September 11th.

And then there's ISIS. I have a simple message for them. Their days are numbered. I won't tell them where and I won't tell them how. We must as, a nation, be more unpredictable. But they're going to be gone. And soon.

Donald Trump is not going to allow our immigration policy to become a Trojan Horse for Radical Islamists. Also, he's going to eradicate ISIS from the face of the earth. Unlike Bush who announced our invasion of Afghanistan weeks in advance, or Hillary who wants him to give his strategy away ahead of time, Trump, like any great military commander, will keep secret his strategy for eradicating ISIS and we will know what it is when he puts it into action.

Secondly, we have to rebuild our military and our economy.
The Russians and Chinese have rapidly expanded their military capability, but look what's happened to us!

Our nuclear weapons arsenal – our ultimate deterrent – has been allowed to atrophy and is desperately in need of modernization and renewal.

Our active duty armed forces have shrunk from 2 million in 1991 to about 1.3 million today. The Navy has shrunk from over 500 ships to 272 ships during that time. The Air Force is about 1/3 smaller than 1991. Pilots are flying B-52s in combat missions today which are older than most people in this room.

And what are we doing about this? President Obama has proposed a 2017 defense budget that, in real dollars, cuts nearly 25% from what we were spending in 2011.

Our military is depleted, and we're asking our generals and military leaders to worry about global warming.

We will spend what we need to rebuild our military. It is the cheapest investment we can make. We will develop, build and purchase the best equipment known to mankind. Our military dominance must be unquestioned.

The US needs to have a military which will dominate any rival military force. We need new airplanes, not airplanes that we used in WWII. Our nuclear arsenal is aged and in need of restoration. We do not want ever to have to use our nuclear weapons, but we must keep up with the Russians and any other world power which has nuclear weapons they can fire at the United States. Although Trump's aim is peace, a strong military and a solid nuclear arsenal will be key components in his plan to bring peace to our planet.

But we will look for savings and spend our money wisely. In this time of mounting debt, not one dollar can be wasted. We are also going to have to change our trade, immigration and economic policies to make our economy strong again – and to put Americans first again. This will ensure that our own workers, right here in America, get the jobs and higher pay that will grow our tax revenue and increase our economic might as a nation. We need to think smarter about areas where our technological superiority gives us an edge. This includes 3-D printing, artificial intelligence and cyberwarfare.

A great country also takes care of its warriors. Our commitment to them is absolute. A Trump Administration will give our service men and women the best equipment and support in the world when they serve, and the best care in the world when they return as veterans to civilian life.

We need to be much more careful with how we spend our dollars on our military systems. In this, the Russians, with much less money at their disposal, have outdone us. Their newest fighter jets are performing magnificently in Syria while our "newest" fighter jets are not performing well enough to be put into production.

Developing new trade policies that put the emphasis on creating high paying jobs here in the United States must be an aim of every trade negotiation. We cannot afford any more NAFTA catastrophes. We need jobs to get the economy going, to increase our economic might as a nation, and to end the feeling of depression that is nationwide. One spinoff from good jobs and a vibrant economy is that tax payments will increase to allow cities, states, and our federal government to fix schools, roads, and will pay down their debts.

Finally we need a Marshall Plan to rebuild our Veterans' Administration and the hospitals and medical care that it oversees. Vets have come back from Korea, Vietnam, Iraq and elsewhere with physical as well as psychological wounds.

We must treat these so well that not one more Vet commits suicide, which has become a weekly scandal. We cannot let this happen ever again.

Finally, we must develop a foreign policy based on American interests.

Businesses do not succeed when they lose sight of their core interests and neither do countries. Look at what happened in the 1990s. Our embassies in Kenya and Tanzania were attacked and seventeen brave sailors were killed on the USS Cole. And what did we do? It seemed we put more effort into adding China to the World Trade Organization – which has been a disaster for the United States – than into stopping Al Qaeda.

We even had an opportunity to take out Osama Bin Laden, and didn't do it. And then, we got hit at the World Trade Center and the Pentagon, the worst attack on our country in its history.

Our foreign policy goals must be based on America's core national security interests, and the following will be my priorities. In the Middle East, our goals must be to defeat terrorists and promote regional stability, not radical change. We need to be clear-sighted about the groups that will never be anything other than enemies.   And we must only be generous to those that prove they are our friends.

Who are our friends in the Middle East? People like Hillary Clinton point to Israel, but what friend would try to sink a US ship? Israeli Air Force jet fighter aircraft and Israeli Navy motor torpedo boats, on 8 June 1967, attacked the United States Navy technical research ship, USS Liberty.   The attack was intentional and the Israelis knew it was an American ship. One Israeli pilot was quoted as saying it was an American ship and he wouldn't fire, so he was called back and jailed. The combined air and sea attack killed 34 crew members (naval officers, seamen, two marines, and one civilian), wounded 171 crew members, and severely damaged the ship.

In May 1968, the Israeli government paid US$3,323,500 in compensation to the families of the 34 men killed in the attack. In March 1969, Israel paid a further $3,566,457 to the *men who had been wounded. On 18 December 1980, Israel agreed to pay $6 million as settlement for the final U.S. bill of $17,132,709 for material damage to Liberty herself plus 13 years' interest.*

There is no doubt that Israel has fessed up to the crime of intentionally trying to sink and American ship. What is pitiful is the response of the American government to this confession: officially it is still an "accident." What makes Israel so special that we give the country over $3 Billion every January and overlook a hostile military action against an American ship that killed US personell?

We desire to live peacefully and in friendship with Russia and China. We have serious differences with these two nations, and must regard them with open eyes. But we are not bound to be adversaries. We should seek common ground based on shared interests. Russia, for instance, has also seen the horror of Islamic terrorism.

I believe an easing of tensions and improved relations with Russia – from a position of strength – is possible. Common sense says this cycle of hostility must end. Some say the Russians won't be reasonable. I intend to find out. If we can't make a good deal for America, then we will quickly walk from the table.

Fixing our relations with China is another important step towards a prosperous century. China respects strength, and by letting them take advantage of us economically, we have lost all of their respect. We have a massive trade deficit with China, a deficit we must find a way, quickly, to balance.

A strong and smart America is an America that will find a better friend in China. We can both benefit or we can both go our separate ways.

The reason for the tension between the USA and Russia is the US leadership has been unable to accept Russia as an equal partner.

Washington politicians are adamant that the US be the "world leader" and the "indispensable nation," even as US influence steadily wanes in the wake of Iraq, Afghanistan, Libya, Syria, Yemen and the Ukraine. Neither Russia, nor China, nor most other countries are willing to accept US leadership, though all are willing to work with the US to solve many of the world's problems, including terrorism.

After I am elected President, I will also call for a summit with our NATO allies, and a separate summit with our Asian allies. In these summits, we will not only discuss a rebalancing of financial commitments, but take a fresh look at how we can adopt new strategies for tackling our common challenges.

For instance, we will discuss how we can upgrade NATO's outdated mission and structure – grown out of the Cold War – to confront our shared challenges, including migration and Islamic terrorism.

I will not hesitate to deploy military force when there is no alternative. But if America fights, it must fight to win. I will never send our finest into battle unless necessary – and will only do so if we have a plan for victory.

Our goal is peace and prosperity, not war and destruction.

Donald Trump knows that NATO is outdated. There are several possible ways NATO can be changed. One would be to include all the nations that are close to the North Atlantic, including Russia. That would end a lot of unnecessary military tension. Another, which might make more sense, would be to dissolve NATO if its mission has been accomplished. "Mission accomplished" is always a good reason for ending an organization.

The thought that we will only deploy our troops when we have a plan for victory seems commonsensical, but it has been far from that under Obama-Clinton's foreign policy. Sending 50, 000 American troops into Afghanistan was criminal, as ghastly as the "Charge of the Light Brigade" which was doomed before the first bugle was sounded. There was neither plan nor hope for victory in Afghanistan and both Obama and Clinton should be held responsible for the loss of limb and life and the wasted pelf.

Finally, it is refreshing to have a president tell us that the goal of our foreign policy is "peace and prosperity." Neither of these has been the goal of US foreign policy military actions since WWII. This change is long overdue. Our military adventures in Afghanistan, Iraq, Libya and elsewhere the past decade, as well as our foolish embrace of the Korean war, were not for "peace and prosperity" and were, instead, an insult to the American military who were wounded or killed in these operations and to their families, friends and communities which suffered the intense grief of the loss of loved ones.

The best way to achieve those goals is through a disciplined, deliberate and consistent foreign policy.

With President Obama and Secretary Clinton we've had the exact opposite: a reckless, rudderless and aimless foreign policy – one that has blazed a path of destruction in its wake.

After losing thousands of lives and spending trillions of dollars, we are in far worse shape now in the Middle East than ever before.

I challenge anyone to explain the strategic foreign policy vision of Obama-Clinton – it has been a complete and total disaster.

I will also be prepared to deploy America's economic resources. Financial leverage and sanctions can be very persuasive – but we need to use them selectively and with determination. Our power will be used if others do not play by the rules.

Our friends and enemies must know that if I draw a line in the sand, I will enforce it.

One of the counter-productive and tension-provoking actions by the Obama administration, encouraged by the neocons who have metastasized throughout the administration and in the State Department (thanks to Hilliar), has been the continual application of sanctions against Russia even though Russian policy improved and has not in any way been anti-American or anti-European. This abuse of sanctions, and also their lack of any effect on Russia, has been one more puzzling feature of the foreign policy under Obama. The intent, perhaps, has been to provoke Putin and Russia, but Putin is for too smart for that childish game.

However, unlike other candidates for the presidency, war and aggression will not be my first instinct. You cannot have a foreign policy without diplomacy. A superpower understands that caution and restraint are signs of strength.

Although not in government service, I was totally against the War in Iraq, saying for many years that it would destabilize the Middle East. Sadly, I was correct, and the biggest beneficiary was Iran, who is systematically taking over Iraq and gaining access to their rich oil reserves – something it has wanted to do for decades. And now, to top it all off, we have ISIS.

My goal is to establish a foreign policy that will endure for several generations. That is why I will also look for talented experts with new approaches, and practical ideas, rather than surrounding myself with those who have perfect resumes but very little to brag about except responsibility for a long history of failed policies and continued losses at war. Finally, I will work with our allies to reinvigorate Western values and institutions.

Instead of trying to spread "universal values" that not everyone shares, we should understand that strengthening and promoting Western civilization and its accomplishments will do more to inspire positive reforms around the world than military interventions.

The good example of strengthening and advertising Western civilization and its accomplishments can inspire positive reforms around the world much more effectively than military interventions, which are typically counter-productive (witness the rise of bin Laden in opposition to our putting troops in Saudi Arabia and our knee-jerk supports of Israel).

Military action is referred to as "hard power." The ability of hard power to create change is limited to the sphere of its coercive reach. The alternative is "soft power." Soft power doesn't create enemies and can have a wide and influential reach. Think of the power of the Vatican to influence public policies across the globe. That is soft power in action. The Vatican has no military but tremendous influence because of the respect people have for it. Likewise, the Dali Lama has great influence without any military involved. That's soft power in action.

Between the end of World War II and the middle of the Vietnam War, the United States wielded significant soft power. That has been spent due to the ineffectual and murderous foreign military policies of Bill Clinton, George Bush II, and Barack Obama. It is time the United States took the high road.

These are my goals, as president.
I will seek a foreign policy that all Americans, whatever their party, can support, and which our friends and allies will respect and welcome.

The world must know that we do not go abroad in search of enemies, that we are always happy when old enemies become friends, and when old friends become allies.

To achieve these goals, Americans must have confidence in their country and its leadership again.

Many Americans must wonder why our politicians seem more interested in defending the borders of foreign countries than their own.

Americans must know that we are putting the American people first again. On trade, on immigration, on foreign policy – the jobs, incomes and security of the American worker will always be my first priority.

No country has ever prospered that failed to put its own interests first. Both our friends and enemies put their countries above ours and we, while being fair to them, must do the same.

This is a huge pivot in foreign policy. We fought the first Iraq war over a boundary dispute between Iraq and Kuwait. What had that to do with the interests of Americans or America? Currently we have troops in Afghanistan, Yemen, Iraq and Syria but for what purpose? Whose interests are they serving? Yet our nation brings home her wounded and dead from these foreign countries and wants the families of these martyrs to think they were serving their country, which is nonsense. As president Donald Trump will only put Americans at risk if there is some actual danger to America and Americans.

By putting American interests first, we will be great again.

We will no longer surrender this country, or its people, to the false song of globalism.

The nation-state remains the true foundation for happiness and harmony. I am skeptical of international unions that tie us up and bring America down, and will never enter America into any agreement that reduces our ability to control our own affairs.

NAFTA, as an example, has been a total disaster for the U.S. and has emptied our states of our manufacturing and our jobs. Never again. Only the reverse will happen. We will keep our jobs and bring in new ones. Their will be consequences for companies that leave the U.S. only to exploit it later.

Under a Trump Administration, no American citizen will ever again feel that their needs come second to the citizens of foreign countries.

I will view the world through the clear lens of American interests.

'Globalization' has become a buzz word for some of my professional colleagues. They seem not to understand what it means or the harm it can bring. The nation-state is the natural locus for policy and internal harmony. International unions and other "globalization" legal fictions are just that, pretenses for something that in reality is neither necessary nor good.

NAFTA is a good example of the harm from "global" agreements as is the Trans-Pacific Partnership (TPP). Hillary Clinton, in 2012, declared that the "TPP sets the gold standard in trade agreements to open free, transparent, fair trade." In fact, the TPP would establish a global governing commission that has been described as a "Pacific Union" comparable to the "nascent European Union" which the British fled when they voted Brexit.

President Trump insists that American interests come first.

I will be America's greatest defender and most loyal champion. We will not apologize for becoming successful again, but will instead embrace the unique heritage that makes us who we are.

The world is most peaceful, and most prosperous, when America is strongest.

America will continually play the role of peacemaker.

We will always help to save lives and, indeed, humanity itself. But to play that role, we must make America strong again.

We must make America respected again. And we must make America great again.

If we do that, perhaps this century can be the most peaceful and prosperous the world has ever known. Thank you.

These are the most profound passages in Donald Trump's speech, though they rely fully on what he has already said.

As president, he will be our champion. We will again be strong and that will help the rest of the world be more peaceful and prosperous.

Donald Trump tells us that "perhaps this century can be the most peaceful and prosperous the world has ever known."

Despite a world of military chaos and cross-currents of conflicting policies, as well as serious military conflicts in Afghanistan, Syria and Iraq, President Donald Trump will do his best to bring about the most peaceful and prosperous century since the Birth of Christ.

CHAPTER SIX
GEORGE WASHINGTON
& "AMERICA FIRST"

"War is the common harvest of all those who participate in the division and expenditure of public money, in all countries. It is the art of conquering at home; the object of it is an increase of revenue; and as revenue cannot be increased without taxes, a pretense must be made for expenditure. . . .Taxes are not

raised to carry on wars, but wars are raised to carry on taxes."

"Whatever is the cause of taxes to a Nation becomes also the means of revenue to Government. Every war terminates with an addition of taxes, and consequently with an addition of revenue; and in any event of war…the power and interest of Governments are increased. War, therefore, as it easily furnishes the presence of necessity for taxes and appointments to places and offices, becomes a principal part of the system of Governments; and to establish any mode to abolish war, however advantageous it might be [to the people], would be to take from such Government the most lucrative of its branches." –Thomas Paine

"The meaning of a word is its use," Ludwig Wittgenstein taught us. The meaning of "America First" seems fairly clear: the government is to institute policies and take actions that benefit our nation and the great majority of those who are its citizens. In addition, the government is not to institute policies or take actions that benefit other nations, other entities, or elites at the cost of reducing benefit to our nation or to the great majority of citizens. Although that is straightforward, critics of America First have misunderstood its implications. My suspicion is that these misunderstandings were deliberate in order to muddy the waters so that we the majority would not take America First seriously The people in the top 1% see America First as very radical and to be suppressed. Although radical in 2016, America First was not radical in 1776 and during the years of George Washington's presidency. The only folks who saw America First as radical in the eighteenth century were the English, who foolishly refused to treat the colonialists as equals and so the Revolutionary War ensued. Our first president did not see America First as radical but rather as the guiding light for the government and the people.

President George Washington decided to forgo a third term, although he had the option, and left the presidency after his second term. With the assistance of Alexander Hamilton and James Madison, Washington wrote a Farewell Address that he never delivered as a public speech but which the *Philadelphia Daily American Advertiser* published on September 19, 1796. This address was subsequently published in all the newspapers around the country. His Farewell Address, a thorough statement of America First, draws out important policy implications. In particular, Washington painstakingly identified two major threats to our young nation.

Washington states clearly the central importance of the power and right of the people as the basis of government:

> The basis of our political systems is the right of the people to make and to alter their

constitutions of government. But **the Constitution which at any time exists**, until changed by an explicit and authentic act of the whole people, **is sacredly obligatory upon all. The very idea of the power and the right of the people to establish government presupposes the duty of every individual to obey the established government.** [GW, 13; emphasizes mine]

As Washington tells us, the very basis of our political system rests on the will of the "whole people." The "whole people" does not mean a consensus or a 100% support by all those who can vote, but a "majority of citizens who do vote." Once he sets out the principle of America First, Washington begins to warn us of the threats to our system of a government whose foundation is the democratic will of the people.

Political Parties are a Threat to the Power of the People

The first threat Washington warns us against will surprise most readers. Washington knew of the dangers of what we now refer to as political parties and how they usurp our power as citizens in a democracy. We see that in the most recent election cycle where the powers-that-be did not want Trump to be the Republican candidate, did not want Bernie Sanders to be the Democratic candidate, and certainly did not want Candidate Donald Trump to win the election.

> All combinations and associations under whatever plausible character with the real design to direct, control, counteract, or awe the regular deliberation and action of the constituted authorities, are destructive of this fundamental principle and of fatal tendency. They serve to organize faction; to give it an

artificial and extraordinary force; to put in the place of the delegated will of the nation the will of a party, **often a small but artful and enterprising minority of the community**; and, according to the alternate triumphs of different parties, to make the public administration the mirror of the ill concerted and incongruous projects of faction, rather than the organ of consistent and wholesome plans digested by common councils and modified by mutual interests. However combinations or associations of the above description may now and then answer popular ends, they are likely, in the course of time and things, to **become potent engines by which cunning, ambitious, and unprincipled men [and women] will be enabled to subvert the power of the people and to usurp for themselves the reins of government,** destroying afterwards the very

engines which have lifted them to unjust
dominion. [GW, 14, emphasis added]

Today we take as a "okay" what Washington saw
as a threat to our power as a people. Few
Americans today find political parties themselves
a threat to democracy. Yet to watch the primary
struggles of Donald Trump and of Bernie Sanders
is to watch a struggle between them and their own
party's elite. Both Trump and Sanders faced
"cunning, ambitious, and unprincipled men [and
women] . . . enabled to subvert the power of the
people and to usurp for themselves the reins of
government." Had the democracy of the
primaries determined the Democrat candidate,
Bernie Sanders would have been the Democrat
candidate for POTUS. Instead, superdelegates,
coin tosses, and other shenanigans came in and
denied the nomination to Sanders and his 12
million followers. Trump was able to struggle
through to the end and become the Republican

candidate. Since the election, the Deep State has been attacking the rebel candidate who threatens to overthrow the status quo.

Washington takes the danger of political parties as a most serious threat:

> Let me now take a more comprehensive view and warn you in the most solemn manner against the baneful effects of the spirit of party, generally.... It exists under different shapes in all governments, more or less stifled, controlled, or repressed....

> The alternate domination of one faction over another, sharpened by the spirit of revenge natural to party dissension, which in different ages and countries has perpetrated the most horrid enormities, is itself a frightful despotism. But this leads at length to a more formal and permanent despotism. . . and

sooner or later the chief of some prevailing faction, more able or more fortunate than his competitors, turns this disposition to the purposes of his own elevation on the ruins of public liberty.

Without looking forward to an extremity of this kind (which nevertheless ought not to be entirely out of sight) the common and continual mischiefs of the spirit of party are sufficient to make it the interest and the duty of a wise people to discourage and restrain it. It serves always to distract the public councils and enfeeble the public administration. It agitates the community with ill-founded jealousies and false alarms, kindles the animosity of one part against another…

Today we have the extremity of the mischiefs of two powerful parties, the Democrats and the Republicans. At the upper levels, hidden often from the public eye, they push for the same aims, namely, to keep themselves in power and keep the people distracted and divided. Dividing the American people has proven most effective until the election of Donald Trump.

Julius Caesar showed us twenty centuries ago that the way to conquer a people is to "divide and conquer," and that is exactly what the two party systems does today. The elites divide us along the lines of race, sexual orientation, employment status, and uses issues like abortion, legalization of marijuana, capital punishment, school prayer, and other hot button social issues to keep us even farther divided and fighting among ourselves. As long as we are a people divided, we are slaves to the machinations of the upper 1% who control the media and both parties. While Hilliar was the Establishment candidate, her political Machine (NOT "team") included almost all the media: NYT, Washington Post, CNN, MSM, and much more). As a result, it was and continues to be nearly impossible for each of us not to have at least one false belief about Trump (he's unreliable, he flies off the handle, he can't be trusted with the nuclear code, he bad mouths women, he knows nothing about leading, he's allowed workers and companies to finish a job but never paid for it, he's a chronic liar, he wants war with Russia, and ad nauseam).

Aware citizens have noticed that even as the parties exchange roles in government, there are only negative changes in the economic status of those in the bottom 90%. Foreign policy remains in the hands of the war mongers who put our military personnel at risk in Korea, Vietnam, and most recently in Afghanistan, Iraq, Pakistan, Yemen, Syria, and a long list of other countries whose sovereignty our government overrides. The main policies (not rhetoric) of domestic and foreign policy does not seem to change for the better but continues in roughly the same pattern whichever party holds the Presidency and/or the Congress. For this reason, we may refer to these two parties as the dual faces of "one" party which we call the **Duopoly** and which has the aim of furthering the interests of the-powers-that-be, including the wealthy, the upper ranks of the military, and the military-industrial complex . It doesn't really matter to the upper elites which party candidate is elected—the taxes of the wealthy and of corporations continue to be reduced, wars continue, the nation's infrastructure continues to crumble, unemployment grows in those jobs that can support a family, the public debt of the country continues to reach new astronomical levels, while the water and the environment of the bottom 90% continues to become less and less healthy. Each of the Establishment candidates of the last election worked for the corporations that control our natural resources, our weaponry, and our media.

It's a Duopoly, one set of basic economic and military polities that has two faces: Democrats and Republicans. .

More and more of us have become more disillusioned; more frustrated, and feel more disenfranchised by this Duopoly (the so-called two party system). We the majority of people even vote in fewer numbers partly because, whomever we vote for, the same policies and indignities continue. Currently less than 25% of the citizens of our nation choose the president. As the commander of Apollo 13 said after the explosion on board the space ship heading toward the moon: "Houston, we have a problem." We have a serious problem when such a small percentage of people and families, supported by unscrupulous propaganda, is able to control the reigns of government.

The Threats of Foreign Influence

The second major threat to a government by and of the people is foreign influence. Picking up from the quote just above, Washington introduces party as the road to foreign influence which itself is the vehicle for corruption.

"The common and continual mischiefs of the spirit of party are sufficient to…. [open] **the door to foreign influence and corruption**, which find a facilitated **access to the government itself through the channels of party passion**s. Thus the policy and the will of one country are subjected to the policy and will of another."[GW, 17; my emphasis].

As we pay attention to our own government today, we know that high level administration officials of the Obama administration, including Obama himself, sacrificed resources that could have helped "we the people" and instead used them to benefit a people or a country not our own. Using Hilliar Clinton as an illustration, she has been working for Israel's aims for years. In the 2016 campaign speech before the Israeli Lobby she has promised that1

> **The first choice** is this: **are we prepared to take the U.S./Israel alliance to the next level? This relationship has always been stronger and deeper than the headlines might lead you to believe.** [Emphasis mine]

Hilliar Clinton not only wants to tighten this attachment to a foreign power, she tells us that this relationship is even more profound than the media is telling us. Hilliar Clinton repeats her question about the "first choice" Americans face in reflecting on the American and Israeli relationship and fills in some of what a positive answer entails from her perspective:

> The United States and Israel must be closer than ever, stronger than ever and more

1 The following quotes are from Hillary Clinton's speech before the American Israeli Polical Action Committee (AIPAC). Time Magazine published her entire speech and it can be found online at: <http://time.com/4265947/hillary-clinton-aipac-speech-transcript/ >

determined than ever to prevail against our common adversaries and to advance our shared values…. Americans and Israelis face momentous choices that will shape the future of our relationship and of both our nations. **The first choice** is this: **are we prepared to take the U.S./Israel alliance to the next level?** It's also why, as president, I will make a firm commitment to ensure **Israel maintains its qualitative military edge**. The United States **should provide Israel with the most sophisticated defense technology** so it can deter and stop any threats. [Emphasis mine]

Hilliar Clinton promised to do what is necessary to maintain the military superiority of Israel's military. That costs money. Is that expense, which could be used to support jobs here in America, consistent with an America First policy? Is it consistent with America First policy to give

333,000 good paying jobs of $90, 000 each to
Israel? Or would it be consistent with America
First policy to keep them here and add another
333,000 jobs to that first batch the following year?
That's over 6,000 of $90,000 jobs per year per
state! Is it in America's interest to give these jobs
to Israel every year? Hilliar also asks:

> The second choice we face is whether we will
> have the strength and commitment to
> confront the adversaries that threaten us,
> especially Iran.

Clinton identifies Iran as a threat to Americans.
On the face of it, this is plainly implausible. Iran
has no nuclear weapons and Tehran is over 6000
miles from Washington, DC. Israeli leaders and
the AIPAC think Iran may eventually produce
nuclear weapons and they prefer Israel to be the
only nuclear power in the Middle East. Clinton

also wonders whether we will stay true to our shared democratic values:

> Will we, as Americans and as Israelis, stay true to the shared democratic values that have always been at the heart of our relationship?

There is great irony in claiming that the USA and Israel even have democratic values. The majority of Americans realize that democracy in America is a myth. We no longer have a government of the people, by the people, for the people. Instead, as a recent study by Princeton University pointed out, "affluent Americans exert substantial influence over the policies adopted by the federal government, and less well-off Americans exert virtually none."2

---

2 Martin Gilens, Affluence and Influence: Economic Inequality and Political Power in America (Princeton University Press, 2012).

Hillary Clinton began her speech by referring to her past work for the benefit of Israel:

> I've had the privilege of working closely with AIPAC members to strengthen and deepen America's ties with Israel.

In her closing remarks, she again tells us that we should grow and deepen the relationship we have had in the past with Israel:

> Let us do the hard work necessary to keep building our friendship and reach out to the next generation of Americans and Israelis so the bonds between our nations grow even deeper and stronger.

Many Americans politicians do not dare to say anything critical of Israel. To criticize Israel for anything having to do with killing Palestinians or stealing land from Palestinians is either anti-

Semitic or, if the critic is Jewish, self-hatred. To avoid any problems with the AIPAC, whose main aim is to foster the interests of Israel even though they are a Political Action Committee fully housed in the USA, most politicians condemn Palestinians for firing occasional missiles into Israel but do not condemn Israel for firing back and killing thousands of Palestinians in return.

There is only one presidential campaigner in the last election who did not traipse to the AIPAC and say something to gain the Jewish vote. Bernie Sanders stands alone in claiming that America should be even-handed in dealing with Israel and with the Palestinians. To the extent that America First implies no favoritism for one nation over another, that would be the policy an American Firster would adopt and publicize, as Washington advises us in his Farewell Address:

Observe good faith and justice towards all nations; cultivate peace and harmony with all; religion and morality enjoin this conduct, and can it be that good policy does not equally enjoin it? It will be worthy of a free, enlightened, and, at no distant period, a great nation, to give to mankind the magnanimous and too novel example of a people always guided by an exalted justice and benevolence. (GW, 22)

Washington warns that permanent hatred of another nation or permanent attachments and fondness to yet other nations puts our nation into the role of a servant or slave of the other nation:

Nothing is more essential than those permanent, inveterate antipathies against particular nations and passionate attachments for others should be excluded and that in place of them just and amicable feelings towards all should be cultivated. The nation which indulges towards another a habitual hatred, or a habitual fondness, is in some degree a slave. (GW, 23)

Against the insidious wiles of foreign influence (I conjure you to believe me, fellow citizens) the jealousy of a free people ought to be constantly awake, since history and experience prove that foreign influence is one of the most baneful foes of republican government. But that jealousy to be useful must be impartial; else it becomes the instrument of the very influence to be avoided, instead of a defense against it. Excessive partiality for one foreign nation and excessive dislike of another cause those whom they actuate to see danger only on one side, and serve to veil and even second the arts of influence on the other. Real patriots, who may resist the intrigues of the favorite, are liable to become suspected and odious, while its tools and dupes usurp the applause and confidence of the people to surrender their interests. (GW, 25-26)

Washington favors extending our trade relations but warns against political entanglements:

The great rule of conduct for us in regard to foreign nations is, in extending our commercial relations, to have with them as little political connection as possible. So far as we have already formed engagements, let them be fulfilled with perfect good faith. Here let us stop. (GW, 26)

It is our true policy to steer clear of permanent alliances with any portion of the foreign world so far, I mean, as we are now at liberty to do it, for let me not be understood as capable of patronizing infidelity to existing engagements (I hold the maxim no less applicable to public than to private affairs, that honesty is always the best policy). (GW, 26)

I repeat . . . let those engagements be observed in their genuine sense. But in my opinion it is unnecessary and would be unwise to extend them. Taking care always to keep ourselves, by suitable establishments, on a respectably defensive posture, we may safely trust to temporary alliances for extraordinary emergencies. Harmony, liberal intercourse with all nations, is recommended by policy, humanity, and interest. But even our commercial policy should hold an equal and impartial hand: neither seeking nor granting exclusive favors or preferences; consulting the natural course of things; diffusing and diversifying by gentle means the streams of commerce but forcing nothing; establishing with powers so disposed in order to give to trade a stable course, to define the rights of our merchants, and to enable the government to support them. (GW, 27-28)

Be a Neutral Nation

The passages above imply that Washington thinks neutrality is part of the America First perspective and he makes it explicit that the USA should be a neutral nation.

> The duty of holding a neutral conduct may be inferred, without anything more, from the obligation which justice and humanity impose on every nation, in cases in which it is free to act, to maintain inviolate the relations of peace and amity towards other nations. (GW, 31)

He applies these principles to the continuing wars in Europe:

> In relation to the still subsisting war in Europe, my proclamation of the 22d of April 1793 is the index to my plan. Sanctioned by your approving voice and by that of your representatives in both houses of Congress, the spirit of that measure has continually governed me, uninfluenced by any attempts to deter or divert me from it. After deliberate examination with the aid of the best lights I could obtain, I was well satisfied that our country, under all the circumstances of the case, had a right to take and was bound in duty and interest to take a neutral position. Having taken it, I determined, as far as should depend upon me, to maintain it with moderation, perseverance, and firmness. (GW, 30)

This neutrality is not isolationism. Rather it is the neutrality of a Switzerland or a Vatican, each of which plays an active role on the world stage but do not favor one nation over another. Neutrality is the America First position, although it is extremely alien to the war-mongering of today's politicians. The one exception to this is the Libertarians. They too think that the US should keep its nose out of the affairs of other nation. The only nationally known politician who held this view is Ron Paul, the former Congressperson from Texas. Ron Paul believed that it was counterproductive to violate he sovereignty of another nation.

What would it like to be a neutral nation in today's world? We get some sense of what this would be like if imagine that the USA was, along with Switzerland and the Vatican, neutral for the past seventy years. Our nation would be economically stronger had we not spent billions annually on weapon systems and on the cost of fighting overseas. We would not be the most feared nation on earth. Our own people and the peoples of other nations would be safer. There would be fewer victims of wars. By not being carried away with the passions of revenge or insult, we would have been able to steer a clear course. We would be better off as a people, though our arms industries would not be so developed or produce our largest exports. Yet if we look at our country as the great folk singer Woody Guthrie wrote—"from sea to shining sea"—we would see that it is our vast landscapes, our ancient forests, our lakes and rivers and streams, and our extensive fertile farmland that make us exceptional when we compare ourselves to Europe. Using these resources wisely, and relying on the security the Atlantic and Pacific oceans provide, we would have been a prosperous nation, an agricultural nation, and our own citizens and the people of the world would be better off because of this neutrality and wise use of resources.

Should some foreign threat arise, or should we face an emergency that we cannot solve alone, we can enter into temporary alliances to deal with these extraordinary circumstances. George Washington clearly affirmed that option. As he wrote:

> Taking care always to keep ourselves by suitable establishments on a respectable defensive posture, we may safely trust to temporary alliances for extraordinary emergencies.

George Washington embraced "America First" and wanted the nation to move in that direction without breaking any promises or agreements. How far our government has strayed from this policy is clear. Most US citizens would like our nation to be neutral in the way of a Vatican or Switzerland. We have Donald Trump to thank for putting the slogan "America First" into the public arena.

CHAPTER SEVEN

A MILITARY DEFENSE OF AMERICA IN ACCORD WITH CHRISTIAN VALUES

We have a great starting point. Except for the contingent of our military forces that will destroy ISIS beginning soon, all our military people and weapons and military contractors will come home to the Continental USA, except for the few that will make Hawaii and Alaska their home. No one with even half a brain cell would attack us as we would be bristling with arms, airplanes, missiles, military on the ground, in short, we'd be like a porcupine. If someone did attack through the spines, Trump would immediately destroy them. No idle Clinton or Obama threats. Such attackers would clearly be crazy, beyond the reach of nonviolence or Christian love. We'd still be practicing the strictest of Gandhian principles of ahimsa.

Even though I've begun this section mentioning two militarily violent actions---destroying ISIS and destroying any attackers of our in-place domestic military---let me now show that Trump's defense of the United States is as nonviolent as anything Mahatma Gandhi could ever have wished for. I've written the book "On Gandhi" that analyzed Gandhi's ahimsa (literally a=no and himsa=harm: no harm, usually translated in these contexts as "nonviolence"). I defended it against standard ordinary and academic criticisms, and also showed how it worked and why Gandhi introduced it. One of the widespread criticisms of ahimsa is that you can get killed being nonviolent. Of course that's true. What people don't realize is that you can get killed being violent. In fact, in our country, you are much more likely to be killed being violent than being nonviolent.

How does nonviolence work? If it is a one-on-one situation, you need to get the violent person's attention, look them in the eyes, listen to why they are upset and angry, realize that you can identify with their point of view, then quiet them down enough to begin a conversation. If it is one group opposing another group, the nonviolent group simply stands its grounds and fearlessly accepts whatever himsa is thrown at it.

For Gandhi, nonviolence is to be used as a method of social transformation and as a method for transforming one's "enemy." Gandhi introduces two terms that are not English in origin. The first is *Satyagraha* which literally means "truth-force;" though more generally it refers to "nonviolent resistance." A practitioner of "truth force" or nonviolence is referred to as a *Satyagrahi.* For this reason, it is never the intention of a *satyagrahi* to embarrass the wrongdoer. The appeal is never to his fear; it is, must be, always to his heart. The *satyagrahi*'s object is to convert, not to coerce, the wrongdoers. He should avoid artificiality in all his doings. He acts naturally from an inward conviction. (CW 69, 69)

Although Gandhi was able to provide good reasons to the British for leaving India, he knew that appealing to reason typically did not persuade anyone to change.

I have come to this fundamental conclusion that if you want something really important to be done, you must not merely satisfy the reason, you must move the heart also. The appeal of reason is more to the head, but the penetration of the heart comes from suffering. It opens up the inner understanding in man. (CW 48, 189)

Given the nonviolent aim of transformation, we are in a better position to catalogue and appreciate both negative and positive requirements of nonviolence from Gandhi's perspective. The negative requirements of nonviolence or *ahimsa* require "not injuring any living being, whether by body or mind. I may not therefore hurt the person of any wrong doer, or bear any ill will to him and so cause him mental suffering." (CW 13, 295) The positive requirements involve situating nonviolence "in the heart and it must be an inseparable part of our very being" (CW 31, 294):

> In its positive form, *ahimsa* means the largest love, the greatest charity. If I am a follower of *ahimsa*, I must love my enemy. I must apply the same rule to the wrong doer who is

my enemy or a stranger to me, as I would to my wrong-doing father or son. This active *ahimsa* necessarily includes truth and fearlessness. (CW 13, 295)

Note the central role here in Gandhi played by love. This is no accident. Love seems to be the central imperative of a number of perspectives on how to defeat hatred and thereby defeat violence.

The best known text of Buddhism is the Dhammapada, which is a popular text containing many of the ethical teachings of Buddhism. It begins with the famous "Twin Verses" (the first two paragraphs below):

All that we are is the result of what we have thought: it is founded on our thoughts, it is made up of our thoughts. If a man speaks or acts with an evil thought, pain follows him, as the wheel follows the foot of the ox that draws the carriage.

All that we are is the result of what we have thought: it is founded on our thoughts, it is made up of our thoughts. If a man speaks or acts with a pure thought, happiness follows him, like a shadow that never leaves him.

For hatred does not cease by hatred at any time: hatred ceases by love, this is an eternal rule

When we turn to the religion that our nation was founded on, Christianity, we find love at the heart of the new commandment that Jesus added to the Ten Commandments:

A new commandment I give to you, that you love one another, even as I have loved you, that you also love one another. (John 13:34)

In the Ten Commandments, as well as in the central precepts of Buddhism, there are two commandments that we have violated much too often from the inception of our Great Nation:

Commandment Six: Thou Shalt Not Kill;

Commandment Eight: Thou Shalt Not Steal.

It is important to note that the Ten Commandments appear at a number of places in the Quran. Here's Commandments Six and Eight:

> Whether open or secret; take not life, which Allah hath made sacred, except by way of justice and law (sura Al-An'am 6:151)

> And come not nigh to the orphan's property, except to improve it, until he attain the age of full strength; give measure and weight with (full) justice;- no burden do We place on any soul, but that which it can bear (ibid)

The commandments not to kill and not to steal are not only in the Old Testament and in the Quran, but are also explicit in the Buddhist precepts and in the texts of Hinduism. That these prohibitions are so widespread suggests a universality to them. To these prohibitions, Christ added the commandment that we love each other.

Although love is necessary for the practice of Gandhian nonviolence that does not mean that one has to love *what* the other person does. Gandhi distinguished between the *deed* and the *doer* of the deed:

> The doer of the deed, whether good or wicked, always deserves respect or pity as the case may be. "Hate the sin and not the sinner" is a precept which, though easy enough to understand, is rarely practised, and that is why the poison of hatred spreads in the world.

This is an important practical consideration for anyone trying to persuade someone, and Gandhi was clear that we should not vilify opponents:

Vilification of an opponent there can never be. But this does not exclude a truthful characterization of his acts. An opponent is not always a bad man because he opposes. He may be as honourable as we may claim to be and yet there may be vital differences between him and us. (CW 46, 108)

Rather than hatred and vilification, Gandhi required civility. In his experience with nonviolence, Gandhi discovered that civility is often difficult to insure, as he noted in writing about a group of agriculturalists who had rid themselves of fear:

It seemed well-nigh impossible to make them realize the duty of combining civility with fearlessness. Once they had shed the fear of the officials, how could they be stopped from returning their insults? And yet if they resorted to uncivility it would spoil their *satyagraha*, like a drop of arsenic in milk....

Experience has taught me that civility is the most difficult part of *satyagraha*. Civility does not here mean the mere outward gentleness of speech cultivated for the occasion, but an inborn gentleness and desire to do the opponent good. (A V, xxv)

Without civility, the transformative power of nonviolence is lost.

Gandhi thought that nonviolence is not only for the dramatic moments when we face thieves or contribute to a social transformation:

If a person does not observe *ahimsa* in his relations with his neighbours and his associates, he is thousands of miles away from *ahimsa*. A votary of *ahimsa*, therefore, should ask himself every day when retiring: "Did I speak harshly today to any co-worker? ... Did I shirk my duty and throw the burden on my co-worker?... Did I not care even to greet the guest who had arrived?... Did I get angry in the kitchen because the rice was half cooked?" All these are forms of intense violence. If we do not observe *ahimsa* spontaneously in such daily acts, we shall never learn to observe it in other fields and, if at all we seem to observe it, our *ahimsa* will be of little or no value. *Ahimsa* is a great force which is active every moment of our lives. It is felt in our every action and thought. (CW 50, 96)

Gandhi was experimenting with a method that had not, at least in recorded history to that time, been successfully used to free a nation from a colonizing power or to free workers from exploitation. We know more today about the effectiveness of nonviolence. It worked in India. It worked in local struggles with the Nazis in Scandinavia, in the civil rights movement in the United States, in persuading the U.S. government to end the Vietnamese War, in the Philippines, in liberating Poland from the U.S.S.R., in bringing down the Berlin Wall, in ending apartheid in South Africa, and most recently in Yugoslavia. Most of this happened only after Gandhi's death, and it is plausible that none of this would have happened without Gandhi's fifty years of promulgating and experimenting with nonviolence. During Gandhi's lifetime people did not envision nonviolence as a viable method of political transformation and he frequently answered objections against it. One objection is that a nonviolent practitioner can get herself killed. Gandhi responded:

Who enjoys the freedom [afterward] when whole divisions of armed soldiers rush into a hailstorm of bullets to be mown down? But in the case of nonviolence, everybody seems to start with the assumption that the nonviolent method must be set down as a failure unless he himself at least lives to enjoy the success thereof. This is both illogical and invidious.

In *satyagraha* more than in armed warfare, it may be said that we find life by losing it. (CW 72, 234-235)

Another frequently raised objection, then as now, is that nonviolence could not work against the Nazis. Gandhi thought otherwise:

[Nonviolent resisters] would offer themselves unarmed as fodder for the aggressor's cannon.... The unexpected spectacle of endless rows upon rows of men and women simply dying rather than surrender to the will of an aggressor must ultimately melt him and his soldiery. (CW 71, 407)

Some would reply, citing the atrocities in the WWII death camps and the genocide of the Jewish people, that nonviolence would not have worked against Hitler. Yet where people did confront the Nazis with organized nonviolence, as in Denmark, they met with success. This hardly proves that nonviolence would have worked against Hitler's soldiery, but it does strengthen that possibility. It is important to note that Gandhian nonviolence is not a passive resistance that involves people staying in their homes. That kind of *passive* activity has absolutely no chance of stopping advancing soldiery. Instead, Gandhi's image is of men and women, without weapons, *actively confronting and not yielding*:

> [Hitler] and his likes have built upon their invariable experience that men yield to force. Unarmed men, women and children offering nonviolent resistance without any bitterness in them will be a novel experience for them. Who can dare say it is not in their nature to respond to the higher and finer forces? They have the same soul that I have. (CW 67, 405)

In WWII it was far easier psychologically for a soldier to kill people who are trying to kill him than it was to kill unarmed people who are simply in his way. Gandhi's nonviolence would have challenged the individual soldiers who would have been required to do the killing. In our arguments and discussions we tend to forget that almost any soldier would rather be back home with family and friends than risking his or her life. If people resist soldiers with awareness and even consideration for their situation, it is not implausible that the soldiers will come to see them as human beings like themselves and will not open fire upon them. In India during the *satyagrahi* struggle, for example, there were occasions when "opponents threw down their guns and fled--shamed, shaken to their depths by the sign of men who valued the lives of others above their own." In a dramatic refusal to follow orders, the men of the Garhwali Rifles, an Indian unit known for its loyalty, refused a British order to fire on unarmed nonviolent demonstrators, saying: "What have they got? They have neither lathis nor stones. On whom should we fire?

CHAPTER EIGHT
THE POWER OF CHRISTIAN LOVE
AND NONVIOLENCE

The successful use of nonviolence against the Nazis in Denmark involved what Gandhi called "non-cooperation." Gandhi discovered non-cooperation when, during a speech, he needed a plan of action that was broader than a mere boycott. He came up with a plan of action and the word "non-cooperation" to describe it. "The only true resistance to the Government, it therefore seemed to me, was to cease to co-operate with it. Thus I arrived at the word 'non-cooperation.'" (A V, xxxvi) During the speech he did not fully appreciate the potential of non-cooperation but intuitively understood that "it is an inalienable right of the people thus to withhold cooperation." (A V, xxxvi) Later, Gandhi wrote about the potential of non-cooperation:

> Imagine a whole people unwilling to conform to the laws of the legislature and prepared to suffer the consequences of non-compliance. They will bring the whole legislative and executive machinery to a standstill. The police and the military are of use to coerce minorities however powerful they may be. But no police or military coercion can bend the resolute will of a people who are out for suffering to the uttermost. (CW75, 148)

If a people are willing to bear the burden of suffering, non-cooperation is a viable method for bringing about transformative change. To Gandhi this made perfect sense: those who want change should bear the suffering necessary to create the change.

For Gandhi, this was not only the way to behave in a large-scale action against those who would exploit us, but also the way to confront aggressors even in our own homes. Gandhi's example involved thieves:

> We punish thieves, because we think they harass us. They may leave us alone, but they will only transfer their attentions to another victim. This other victim however is also a human being, ourselves in a different form, and so we are caught in a vicious circle. The trouble from thieves continues to increase, as they think it is their business to steal. In the end we see that it is better to endure the thieves

than to punish them. The forbearance may even bring them to their senses. By enduring them we realize that thieves are not different from ourselves, they are our brethren, our friends, and may not be punished. But whilst we may bear with the thieves, we may not endure the infliction. That would only induce cowardice. So we realize a further duty. Since we regard the thieves as our kith and kin, they must be made to realize the kinship. And so we must take pains to devise ways and means of winning them over. This is the path of ahimsa. It may entail continuous suffering and the cultivating of endless patience. Given these two conditions, the thief is bound in the end to turn away from his evil ways. Thus step by step we learn how to make friends with the entire world. (CW 44, 58)

The point is to help the thief see that we are like him and like him we suffer when he steals our things. If we threaten the thief with prison, or with death, of course he may agree not to steal, at least from us. But he is still a thief. Coercion generally does not alter a person's attitudes or habits. "All true change comes from within," Gandhi noted. "Any change brought about by pressure is worthless." (CW 83, 317).

There has been a Christian nonviolent movement in this country opposing war and capital punishment. There are a number of active Christian antiwar organizations:

- American Friends Service Committee.
- Anglican Pacifist Fellowship.
- Catholic Association for International Peace.
- Catholic Worker Movement.
- Christian Peace Conference.
- Episcopal Peace Fellowship.
- Fellowship of Reconciliation.

- Friends Committee on National
  Legislation.

Some of the best known Christian antiwar
activists include, Leo Tolstoy, Ammon Hennacy,
Martin Luther King, Daniel Berrigan and Philip
Berrigan. In this list I knew nothing of Ammon
Hennacy. Ammon Ashford Hennacy (July 24,
1893 – January 14, 1970) was an Irish-American
pacifist, Christian anarchist, social activist,
member of the Catholic Worker Movement and a
Wobbly. He established the "Joe Hill House of
Hospitality" in Salt Lake City, Utah and practiced
tax resistance. Although the US government does
not celebrate Martin Luther King as an antiwar
activist, he became a fully motivated critic of the
Vietnamese War which cost him some of the
white support he had up until the last year of his
life. Some people believe that it was his vocal
opposition to the war which was the ultimate
motivation for his assassination.

Ismael Hossein-Zadeh says the current military and racial policies of the US go back at least forty years. I think they go all the way back to President Dwight Eisenhower, who basically catalyzed the Vietnamese War by denying Ho Chi Ming the presidency of a united Vietnam. In his Farewell Address, Eisenhower warned us about the military-industrial-political complex (usually we only hear about the "military-industrial complex" but in the draft of the speech he wrote all three and just felt too gentlemanly to criticize the political class to its face). President Kennedy was trying to pull us out of the war in Vietnam and back from the Jim Crow racism that characterized most of the country when he was assassinated.

Neither Eisenhower nor JFK were owned by the Establishment and neither thought of himself as an Establishment lackey. JFK stood up to the Joint Chiefs of Staff, his Secretary of Defense and his brother Bobby, the Secretary of State, in refusing to go along with their consensus that the Cuban missile crisis required that the US should invade Cuba because the Russians were siting long range missiles, six of which could reach our major cities with nuclear warheads. As a result, during those tense days and nights, Kennedy was skillfully able to side step a nuclear war with Russia and the Russians took the missiles out of Cuba.

JFK was interested in ways of radically improving race relations and was in close contact with Martin Luther King. He was about to pull us out of the Vietnamese war. He blamed the CIA for the Bay of Pigs fiasco and promised to break it into a thousand pieces. In these and other ways he became a threat to an Establishment that benefited from war and racism. He was assassinated. His brother Bobby Kennedy was assassinated. Black leader Malcom X was assassinated. Martin Luther King was assassinated. The Vietnamese war blew up in our faces and we were defeated, which couldn't be blamed on anyone except the lies on which it was based and an anti-war movement that was a grassroots-up and fueled by a new wave of Democracy that the Establishment found difficult to manage and has done its best to crush ever since (until the Occupy Movement, which was crushed by a unified action of police across the country). I think both the Bernie Sanders wave of supporters and the Donald Trump wave of supporters are recent incarnations of grass-roots democracy energy. The Hillary Clinton MACHINE [not "team," but a Machine including major governmental forces—POTUS Obama, the Attorney General, and the Federal Reserve--- major news outlets both in print (NYT, Wash Post, UK's Guardian) and on television (CNN takes the cake here for firing Dr. Drew who made a medical report on Hillary Clinton's health based on a medical report her doctor had released), plus all the big money-makers… the Clinton MACHINE that included every Establishment organization and presstitute continues to do its best to crush Donald Trump through rumor and innuendo. This book sets Donald Trump's record straight.

At its heart nonviolence is as Christian as Jesus' commandment that we love one another. Why does a Christian nation have such difficulty with policies that prohibit killing? Why did Hilliar Clinton delight in the destruction of Libya and the murder of Gadhafi? Why was president Obama so willing to use drones when he knew that they more often than not kill innocent men, women and children?

While there are answers to these questions, the biggest question is why do we, who are reading this book, think that it is perfectly alright to live in a nation that attacks other nations, kills thousands of innocents, and carries on like this was as good and right as having Thanksgiving Dinner?

There are several reasons. First, most people have never thought through what you have just read. Nonviolence isn't "American" even if it is Christian. Wouldn't nonviolence *prohibit* the ownership of guns? Absolutely not. Wouldn't it wipe out the profits of the Military-industrial complex? After all, killing tools and machines are the biggest export of the USA. Wouldn't the NRA raise an eyebrow?

First, nonviolence between humans would not prohibit the private ownership of guns. Forget the fact that they are needed for hunting or that shooting is now part of the Olympics or that we need them to re-create dramatic historical military events in our nation's history. Most of us don't trust the government, couldn't trust any of the governments under the Bush, the Clintons, or Obama. We want guns to protect our families and neighborhoods from government and other crazies. As the bumpersticker says, "you can have my gun when you can pry it from my cold dead fingers." So, no, even in a nation professing Christs teachings, guns have an important role to play. But, you ask, aren't lots of innocents killed every year because of guns? I'm sure they are, but aren't a lot of innocents killed every year because of cars?

We will have military units in the USA, Alaska and Hawaii. We will need the newest and best weaponry, airplanes, and so forth. So our own military-industrial corporations can compete on the world market to supply our own military with the best of military equipment. We don't want to purchase from a company just because it's American. We will purchase the very best that is for sale. But might not some companies go out of business because they aren't' competitive with a Chinese factory? Well, then they go out of business. We're looking to satisfy the criterion "America First."   But if an American corporation goes bankrupt, that's a loss of jobs and a Congressman will be annoyed because it's in his district.   That's where Trump's great jobs program will fill the bill.   Well, if we are closing bases on because of America First, Trump's job program will not replace a whole military city of workers.   That's true but military bases are notoriously environmentally dirty---years of spilt fuels and toxins. The government will have to develop clean-up crews of workers getting the same $90K a year to clean up these bases and make them safe for children and animals.

As a model nation for peace we will have to stop exporting small arms, grenades, bombs and other equipment that the Toyota-driving ISIS killers use in their killing businesses.   If you've been thinking of ISIS, you would realize that Gandhi's hope of WWII nonviolence working against

Nazi's would not work against ISIS. These simple nonviolent tactics would also not work against black ops military, snipers who have no lack of appetite to kill people from a half-mile away, drone operators who can kill from office desks in a Las Vegas shelter, and when they do start being affected by PTS and start committing suicide, there's enough volunteers to replace them for as long as we have drones to fly. The same ISIS murderous impulses are true of child soldiers the world over. Killing is a game to them, much as kids in the US play the very realistic video games where they blow bodies into thousands of bloody pieces.

Gandhi had an answer for how to protect people from such killers who were immune to displays of nonviolence. Gandhi thought that there were situations in which a violent defense was required. These are primarily cases of defending innocents from attacks by animals. While Gandhi thought that nonviolent action could persuade persons, he did not think nonviolence would typically persuade an attacking animal. Gandhi also thought that there may be human assailants who are also beyond the reach of persuasion. Gandhi would not consider a human assailant beyond possible persuasion just because he or she was bitter, angry, jealous, fearful, drunk, driven by ideology, full of hatred, a thug, or a professional soldier, for just such assailants were among those Gandhi and other *satyagrahi*s confronted in India and whom nonviolence often persuaded. But if the assailant is a "lunatic" who was furiously "killing anyone who came in his way," Gandhi would agree that it is a duty to use violence against such a "lunatic." (CW 31, 544) The lunatic assailant is as beyond the persuasive power of nonviolence as is the typical nonhuman animal. Except for this very circumspect case, Gandhi held violence is not justifiable against humans even in defense, that we are not to prepare for it, and that it is never to be used to promote social change. In short, Gandhi is promulgating a new paradigm but within this paradigm we have an answer for the lunatic killers who compose ISIS: we simply kill them.

Would Jesus be able to accept this? Think of those whom Jesus as a young man threw out of the temple. There were money changers, the financiers of their day who interacted with Joe Public.   If they were as much into money as the banksters and brokers of today, there was no chance that they would grow spiritually. Scheckels under the mattress was more important than almost anything, even the health of a child or wife. Their attachment to money probably blinded them as it blinded our own money agents to the laws they were breaking in creating the housing bubble that burst in 2008.

Think of what our real estate professionals were doing in this Christian country that produced the bubble. Agents were selling houses to customers who could not afford them; brokers were coming up with loans for buyers who didn't satisfy the loan requirements; lawyers were closing these deals knowing they were not financially viable. But they became so. As the housing market flew to new heights, loans that were not viable a year earlier suddenly became viable because of the value the buyers now had in the house. Although professionals were violating the relevant laws and standards, they could also rationalize that the laws and standards were out of date because look, they were making money and the loans were becoming viable as the value of houses rose. There was no way to buy and sell homes in this overheated market without jumping in and playing the game. Any agent or broker who blew the whistle would have had to look for work in another field where she or he wasn't being black-balled. It was self-sustaining.

Here, in a Christian nation, with "in God we trust" on the dollar bill, almost all financiers were playing real estate roulette. Is there a commandment against that? No, but there is one against stealing and they were all stealing from the last customer to get a mortgage, and from future generations who would feel the effects of the 2008 burst bubble for years to come. All were blinded by the dollar bill, the race to get more, and the bubble got pretty big before it burst and took the whole economy with it. We are still feeling the effects and I doubt that we will climb out until President Trump puts his domestic policies in place.

Jesus saw the blinding effect of money on the human soul. He knew its power and the weakness of men and women who pursued it so he threw the money-lenders out of the temple. Was he angry? While the elders being tossed out by a young man certainly saw it that way, maybe he wasn't.   Maybe he was highly motivated and, being a young man, highly energized, and thrashed at them until they got out. What else would make an otherwise nice young Jewish lad so crazy as to throw his Jewish elders out of their place of business? It wasn't anger. It had to be done.

CHAPTER NINE

THE PEACE AMENDMENT

The parallel between Gandhi's nonviolence, which rests on love, and Jesus's love, which generated throwing the financiers out of the temple, are parallel. Each acknowledges exceptions where love cannot work. It can't work with ISIS which is so blinded by hatred that it will kill until there's no one left to kill. It can't work with financiers so blinded by greed that they will keep going until there's no more money to get. We can think of this section as "returning the nation to Christian values" or, if you prefer, "showing the relevance of Gandhian nonviolence to a more peaceful way of defending the USA."

Although it is amazing to me that President Donald Trump's defense of the United States rests on Christian / Buddhist / Gandhian values, at some point Donald Trump will no longer be president. Thomas Jefferson famously said that "Every generation needs a new revolution." Jefferson also acknowledged the great truth about human nature that eight years of peace will not change: *If once the people become inattentive to the public affairs, you and I, and Congress and Assemblies, Judges and Governors, shall all become wolves. It seems to be the law of our general nature, in spite of individual exceptions.*"

My hope is that Donald Trump will be president through the election of 2024. There will be a new generation of voters to help choose the president following Trump. Likely that president will be a woman. Donald Trump has an incredibly politically astute daughter, Ivanka, who would be a strong contender to become the Republican candidate. The Democrats will have a strong contender for the Democratic nominee in Tulsi Gabbard who is the United States Representative for Hawaii's 2nd congressional district since 2013. She was also a vice-chair of the Democratic National Committee until February 28, 2016, when she resigned in order to endorse Senator Bernie Sanders for the 2016 Democratic presidential nomination. She certainly will have a running start, based on a record of remarkable integrity. She might even challenge President Trump in the 2000 presidential election cycle, though I think, given the quality of woman that she is, she will likely be in the Senate by that time and let Trump's policies, with which I doubt she'll have any trouble, carry on until 2024. Looking that far ahead from 2017, I would think she would be the woman candidate of choice for the Democrats and, if it is two women opposing each other, it will be a remarkable election. All of Hilliar's tired attempts to ride the woman's vote to the presidency will be irrelevant: whichever candidate wins, Republican Trump or Democrat Gabbard, there will be a woman president. Hilliar might have broken into the history books by unfairly manipulating Sanders out of the race, but this post- Donald Trump contest will be the real thing. Two women, of integrity, one of whom will win the election for President of the United States in 2024.

My futuristic intuitions feel awake and, they are also sending out a strong warning signal. As Thomas Jefferson warned, we need a revolution every generation. As he also warned, if the public grows just a little relaxed and less vigilant, human nature suggests that darker forces will begin to grow stronger. For this reason I believe it is important for the Trump Administration to pass a Peace Amendment to the Constitution as quickly as possible. Here is a version of such an amendment. I did not make this up but modified it from one published by Brigadier General Smedley D. Butler, the most decorated American soldier who fought in WWI. In 1936 he published the peace amendment. The aim of the amendment was to keep our young people out of war as well as to "guarantee everlasting peace to our nation." The amendment, if ratified and followed, would take our nation out of the horrific practice, fully condoned by prior candidate Hilliar Clinton, of killing people because they didn't agree that we were to be the Supercops of the Globe. Neither Bernie Sanders nor Donald Trump adopted Hilliar's warmonger theme, and we are very lucky that Candidate Trump won.

The Peace Amendment below is based on General Butler's 1936 amendment but, since this is 80 years later, there will be a few necessary changes. We propose, in the name of Brigadier General Smedley D. Butler, an Amendment for Peace to the Constitution of the United States:

Whereas current constitutional restrictions do not prohibit killing civilians overseas to promote the national welfare, whether these killings promote the national welfare or not, this very deep violation of Christian values needs to be blocked by this amendment to the constitution which document is intended to direct and guide this great Christian nation. Jesus Christ came to earth with two commandments: Honor thy Lord and God and, second, love thy neighbor as thyself. This important teaching does not prohibit us from hating what our neighbor does when he sins or otherwise violates us. Instead, it guides us to hate the sin but love the sinner, much as we find in the ancient texts of Asian religions as well as in the teachings of Mahatma Gandhi.

In order to put our military actions on a Christian foundation, in order to free the world from the violence which US invasions, US arming of combatants, or the US going along with the murders of innocents that other nations like Israel do regularly, we propose an Amendment for Peace to the Constitution of the United States:

1. The removal of members of the land forces of any of our military units from within the continental limits of the United States, Alaska, or Hawaii, to any offshore base, including the removal of armed contractors or others who work with our military when they are in battle, is prohibited.

2. The vessels of any branch of the armed services, or of any contractor who's operating vessels for any military purpose, is prohibited

from sailing for any reason, except on an errand of mercy to a vessel or airplane in distress on the ocean, more than one thousand miles from our coastline, more than one thousand miles from Hawaii, or more than 500 miles from Alaska.

3. Any and all military aircraft, including spy aircraft and contractor aircraft, are hereby prohibited from flying, for any reason whatsoever, more than 1250 miles from beyond the coast of the United States, including Hawaii and 550 miles from the coast of Alaska.

4. The purpose of this amendment is to insure that American military, of whatever ethnic origin or sex, are never sent overseas to be needlessly shot at or shot down in European, Middle Eastern, Far Eastern, Asiatic, Southeast Asian, Australian, New Zealand,

Anarchic or Artic Circle conflicts that are of no concern to our people.

5. The second purpose of this amendment is to bring US military policy in line with Christ's teaching. We will not pretend to be the world's global cop; we will cease immediately droning innocents in the manner of Israel which first introduced us to the extrajudicial assassination and led us too easily into that illegal and immoral practice; we will not hold prisoner anyone from a foreign country for which we lack habeas corpus; we will maintain no prisons or similar facilities anywhere in the world outside of the continental United States, Alaska and Hawaii.

6. We believe that by following this Peace Amendment we can be a beacon for peace and soft power for peace in the world. Our nation will be fully protected from foreign attack. Our law and order domestic police

forces will keep us protected from internal terrorist attack. We will screen all immigrants, as we have in the past, before any of them become citizens. Since we are not a destination for refugees, we will accept refugees only after a fine-tuned and careful screening process that includes close examination of (a) country of origin; (b) reason for leaving; (c) examining for family ties and family tree; (d) a thorough examination for any terrorist connections. (e) We will treat Muslims, atheists, Christians, Jews, Buddhists, Hindus and members of any other religious designation with equal care, equal scrutiny, and equal respect. The aim in any such policy is to protect Americans from those who may want to attack us.

With that amendment in place, President Donald Trump and his women successors can rest assured that the US will be fully defended from attack and yet be a beacon of peace and hope for all humankind.

Bart Gruzalski, fourth from right, with Mary McAfee, President of Ireland, and her husband (left), with an interfaith group.

The author, Bart Gruzalski, with another visitor to the President's Residence, Dublin, Ireland.

ACKNOWLEDGEMENTS

I am especially indebted to my wife Marion for taking care of me as I worked through yet one more book on Trump (she wanted me to write on something else) and for making decisive comments and suggestions that put the title and the text into written harmony. I am also indebted to the Saker who gave me permission to use the article that became Chapter Three and which was the stimulus that motivated me to write this book. Some passages are modified or taken from two other books: *Why Christians and Peace-advocates Must Vote for Trump* and *The Moral Imperative of "America First!": Join November's Nonviolent Christian Revolt against America's Royalty.* I am grateful to Wild Pelican Press LLC for permission to use these passages as I have done.

www.ingramcontent.com/pod-product-compliance
Lightning Source LLC
Chambersburg PA
CBHW032007170526
45157CB00002B/578